The Writings of Eric Harris and Dylan Klebold

Table of Contents

Part I: Eric Harris

Journal

Class of 98,
top of the
"should have died"
list.

I hate this fucking world, to much
god damn fuckers in it. to many thoughts
and different societies all wrapped up together
in this fucking place called AMERICA. everyone
has their own god damn opinion on every god
damn thing. and you may be saying "well
what makes you so different?" because I have
something only me and V have, SELF AWARENESS.
call it existentialism or whatever the fuck I
want. we know what we are to this world
and what everyone else is. we learn more
than what caused the civil war and how to
simplify quadratics in school. we have been
watching you people. we know what you
think and how you act. all talk and
no actions. people who are said to be
brave or courageous are usually just STUPID
then they say later that they did it on purpose
cause they are brave. when they did on fucking
accident. GOD everything's so corrupt and
so filled with opinions and points of view
and peoples own little agendas and skedules.
there isn't a world anymore. its H.O.E. and
(we) know it. self awareness is a

wonderful thing, I know I will die soon, so will you and everyone else. maybe we will be lucky and a comet will smash us back to day 1 people say it's immoral to follow others, they say be a leader. well here is a fukin news flash for you stuped shits, everyone is a follower! everyone who says they arent followers and then dresses diff. or acts diff... they got that from something they saw on TV or in film or in life, NO originality, how many JO MAMMA jokes are there and how many do U think are original and not copied. NONE. it's a fucking filthy place we live in all these standards and laws and Great Expectations (webb) are making people into robots even though they might "think" they arent and try to deny it. no matter how hard I try to NOT copy someone I still AM! except for this fucking piece of paper right here. and B.T.W. spelling is stuped unless I say, I say spell it how it sounds, its the fukin easiest way! hey try this sometime, when someone tells you something, ask "why?" eventually they will be stumped and can't answer any more. that's because they only know what they need to know in society and school, not real life science, they will end up saying words to this "because! Just shut up!!) people that only know stuped facts that arent important should be shot, what fucking use are they. NATURAL SELECTION. Kill all retards, people w/ brain fuck ups, drug adics, people who cant figure out how to use a fucking lighter. Geeeewd! people spend millions of dollars on saving the lives of retards, and why, I don't buy that shit like "oh, he's my son though!" so the fuck what, he aint normal, kill him, put him out of his misery he is only a waste of time and money, then people say "but he is worth the time, he is human too" no he isnt, if he was then he would swallow a bullet cause he would realize what a fucking worthless burden he was. — 4/10/98

As I said before, self awareness is a wonderful thing. I know what all you fuckers are thinking and what to do to piss you off and make you feel bad. I always try to be different, but I always end up copying someone else. I try to be a mixture of different things and styles but when I step outside of myself I end up looking like others or others THINK I am copying. One big fucking problem is people telling me what to fuckin do, think, say, act, and everything else. I'll do what you say IF I feel like it. But people (LE. parents, cops & teachers) telling me what to do just makes me not want to fucking do it! thats why my fucking name is REB (!!) no one is worthy of shit unless I say they are. I feel like God and I wish I was, having everyone being OFFICIALLY lower than me. I already know that I am higher than almost anyone in the fucking welt in terms of universal Intelligence and where we stand in the universe compared to the rest of the UNIV. and if you think I dont know what I'm talking about then you can just "FICK DICH" and saugen mein Hund! Isnt america supposed to be the land of the free? how come, if em free, I cant deprive a stupid fucking dumbshit from his possession? If he leaves them sitting in the front seat of his fucking van out in plain sight and in the middle of fucking nowhere on a Fri fucking day night NATURAL SELECTION! fucker should be shot. same thing with all those rich snotty toadies at my school fuckers think they are higher than me and everyone else with all their $ just because they were born into it? Ich denk NEIN. BTW, "sorry" is just a word. It doesnt mean SHIT to me. everyone should be put to a

test, an ULTIMATE DOOM test, see who can survive
in an environment using only smarts and military skills.
Put them in a doom world. no authority, no refuge, no
BS copout excuses. If you cant figure out the area
of a triangle or what "cation" means, you die!
if you cant take down a demon w/ a chainsaw or
kill a hell prince w/ a shotgun, you die! fucking
snotty rich fuckheads ████████████ who sorta rely
on others or on sympathy or ∄ to get them through
life should be put to this challenge. plus it would
get rid of all the fat, retarded, crippled, stupid, dumb,
ignorant, worthless people of this world. no one
is worthy of this planet, only me and who ever I choose.
there is just no respect for anything higher than
your fucking boss or parent. everyone should be
shot out into space and only the people I say should
be left behind 4/12/98

ever wonder why we go to school? besides getting a so called
education. its not to obvious to most of you stupid fucks but
for those who think a little more and deeper you should realize
it. its societies way of turning all the young people into
good little robots and factory workers, thats why we sit
in desks in rows and go by bell schedules, to get prepared
for the real world 'cause "thats what its like." well god
damit no it isnt! one thing that seperates us from other animals
is the fact that we can carry on actual thoughts. so why dont
we? people go on day by day. rut ine shit. why cant we learn in school
how we want to, why cant we sit on desks and on shelves and put
our feet up and relax while we learn? cause thats not what
the "real world is like" well hey fuckheads, there is no such thing as an
actual "real world", its just another word like justice, sorry, pity, religion,
faith, luck and so on. we are humans, if we dont like something we
have the fucking ability to change! but we dont, atleast U dont, I would
just whine & bitch throughout life but never do a goddam
thing to change anything. "man can eat, drink, fuck, and hunt and
anything else he does is madness" — Based on Lem's quote. boy oh fuckin boy
is that true. when I go NBK, and people say things like, "oh it was so
tragic," or "oh he is crazy!" or "it was so bloody." I think, so the fuck what you,

9

think that's a bad thing? just because your mommy and daddy told you blood and violence is bad, you think it's a fucking law of nature? WRONG, only science and math are true, everything, and I mean Every fucking thing else is Man made. my doctor wants to put me on medication to stop thinking about so many things and to stop being angry. well, I think that anyone who doesn't think like me is just bullshitting themselves. try it sometime if you think you are worthy, which you probly will you little shits, drop all your beliefs and views and ideas that have been burned into your head and try to think about why your here, but I bet most of you fuckers can't even think that deep, so that is why you must be. how dare you think that I and you are part of the same species when we are soooooooo different. you aren't human. you are a Robot. you don't take advantage of your capabilities given to you at birth. you just drop them and hop onto the boat and head down the stream of life with all the other fuckers of your type. well god damnit I won't be a part of it! I have thought to much, realized to much, found out to much, and I am to self aware to just stop what I am thinking and go back to society because what I do and think isn't "right" or "morally accepted." NO, NO, NO God Fucking damnit NO! I will sooner die than betray my own thoughts. but before I leave this worthless place, I will kill whoever I deem unfit for anything at all. especially life. and If you pissed me off in the past, you will die if I see you. because you might be able to piss off others and have it eventually all blow over, but not me. I don't forget people who wronged me, like ██████████ he will never get a chance to read this because he will be dead by me before this is discovered. — 4/21/98

The human race sucks. human nature is smothered out by society, jobs, and work and school. instincts are deleted by laws. I see people say things that contradict themselves, or people that don't take any advantage to the gift of human life. they waste their minds on memorizing the stats of every college basketball player or how many words should be in a report when they should be using their brain on

more important things. the human race isn't worth fighting for anymore. WWII was the last war worth fighting and was the last time human life and human brains did any good any made us proud. now, with the government having scandals and conspiracies all over the fucking place and lying to everyone all the time and with worthless pointless mindless disgraceful TV shows on and with everyone obsessed with hollywood and beauty and fame and glamour and politics and anything famous, people just aren't worth saving. Society may not realize what is happening but I have; you go to school, to get used to studying and learning how you're "supposed to" so that draws or filters out a little bit of human nature. but thats after your parents taught you whats right and wrong even though you may think differently, you still must follow the rules. after school you are expected to get a job or go to college, to have more of your human nature blown out your ass. society trys to make everyone act the same by burying all human nature and instincts. thats what school, laws, jobs, and parents do. if they realize it or not, and them; the few who stick to their natural instincts are casted out as psychos or lunatics or strangers or just plain different. crazy, strange, weird, wild, these words are not bad or degrading. if humans were let to live how we un naturally it would be chaos and anarchy and the human race wouldn't probably last that long, but hey guess what, thats how its supposed to be!!!! society and government are only made to have order and calmness, which is exactly the opposite of pure human nature. take away all your laws and morals and just see what you can do. if the government was one entity it would be thinking " hey, let's make some order here and calm these crazy fucks down so we can be constructive and fight other governments in our own little so called self created "civilized world" and get rid of all those damn instincts everyone has!! well shit I'm to tired to write anymore tonight, so until next time, fuck you all
                                                                    -5/6/98

It has been confirmed, after getting my yearbook and watching people like ██████ and ██████ the human race isn't worth fighting for, only worth killing. give the Earth back to the animals, they deserve it infinitely more than we do. nothing means anything anymore, most quotes are worthless, especially the rearranged ones like "dont fight your enemies, make your enemies fight" you know, quotes that use the same phrase just rearranged, Dumbfuck shit~~yeah~~ woah its funny, people say "you shouldn't be so different." To me, and 1ST I say fuck you dont tell me what I should and should don't be and 2ND mother fuckers different is good, I dont want to be like you or anyone which is almost impossible this day w/ all the little shits trying to be "original-copy cats", I expect shits like you to criticize anyone who isn't one of your social words; "normal" or "civilized" → see: Tempest and Can all you degrading worthless shits. all caught up and brainwashed into the 90's society. "what? you AREN'T going to college, are you crazy!" holy 4 that is one fucking BIG Quote that just proves my point. step back and look at yourself fuckers, I dare you, maybe I'll get lucky and you'll step back too far like Nick in E/M3. w/ the same consequences.
                                                    —5/9/98

wooh, different pen. HA! alright you pathetic fools listen up; I have figured it out. the human race strives for exellence in life and community. always wanting to bring more = good = into the comm. and nulifiy = bad = things. anyone who thinks differently than the majority or the leaders is deemed "unusual" or weird or crazy. people want to be a part of something; a family, a service, a club, a union, a community, whatever. thats what humans want. who cares what you as an individual thinks, you must do what you are told, whether it's er jump off a bridge or drive on the right side of the road. protesters in the past protested because the human race that was dominate (Ghandhi and the Brits or the ki and the Americans) ~~crease~~ wasnt working out = they had fault = they failed = their ideas didnt work. humans dont change that much, they only get better technology to do their work quicker/easier. people always say we shouldn'T be racist. why not? Blacks ARE different. like it or not they are. they started out on the bottom so why not keep em there. it took the centuries to convince us that they are equal but they still use their color as an excuse. or they just ~~we~~ discriminate us because we are white. Fuck you, we should ship yer black asses back to Affri fucking ca were you came from. we brought you here and we will take you back. America = white. Gays.... well all gays, ALL gays, should be killed. m.T frame frozen. lesbians are fun to watch + they are hot but still, its not human. its a Fucking disease. you dont see bulls or roosters trying to fuck do you? no, I didn't think so. women, you will always be under men. its been seen throughout nature, males are almost always doing the dangerous shit while the women stay back. its your animal instincts, deal with it or commit suicide, just do it quick. thats all for now - 5/20/98

"If you recall your history the Nazi's came up with a "final solution" to the Jewish problem... kill them all. well incase you havent figured it out yet, I say,

"KILL MANKIND" no one should survive. we all live in lies. people are always saying they want to live in a perfect society, well utopia doesn't exist. It is human to have flaws... you know what, Fuck it, why should I have to explain myself to you survivors when half of this shit I say you shitheads wont understand and if you can then woopie fuckiny do. that just means you have something to say as my reason for killing. and the majority of the audience wont even understand my emotives either! they'll say "ah, hes crazy, hes insane, oh well, I wonder if the bulls won." you see! It's fucking worthless! all you fuckers should die! DIE what the fuck is the point if only some people see what I am saying, there will always be ones who dont, ones that are to dumb or naive or ignorrant or just plain retarded. If I cant pound it into every single persons head then it is pointless. fuck mercy fuck justice fuck morals fuck civilized fuck rules fuck laws... DIE manmade words... people think they apply to everything when they dont/cant. theres no such thing as True Good or True evil, its all relative to the observer. its just all nature, chemistry, and math. deal with it. but since dealing with it seems impossible for mankind, since we have to slap warning labels on nature, then ... you die, burn, melt, evaporate, decay, just go the fuck away !!!! YAAAAA!!!

- 6/12/98 -

"when in doubt, confuse the hell out of the enemy" - Fly 9/2/98

wait, mercy doesn't exist...

heres something to chew on.... today I saw a program on the discovery channel about satelites and radar and aircraft and stuff, and at the end of the show the narrator said some things that made me think " damn, we are so advanced, we kick ass, america is awesome, we have so many things in our military, we would kick anyones ass." for a minute I actually had some pride in our nation.... then I realized, "hey, this only the Good things that I am seeing here. only the Pros, not the cons. maybe thats what people see, only the Pros, and thats why they are under control, but me, I see all... you can only blind me for so long, but alas, I have realized that Yes, the human race is still indeed doomed. It just needs a few kick starts, like me, and hell, maybe even ████████ If I can whipe a few cities off the map, and even the fuckhead Holding the map, then great. hmm, just thinking if I want ALL humans dead or maybe just the quote-unquote "civilized, developed, and known-of" places on Earth, maybe leave little tribes of natives in the vain forest er something, hmm, I'll think about that. eh, done for tonight ~R|E|B~ -6/13/98-

as part of the human race, and having the great pleasure of being blessed with a brain, I can think. Humans can do whatever they want. There are no laws of nature that prevent humans from making choices. maybe from actually DOING some of those choices, but not from making the choices If a man chooses to speed while driving home one day, then it is his fault for whatever happens. If he crashes into a school bus full of kidies and they all burn to death, its his fault. Its only a tragedy if you think it is, and then its only a tragedy in your own mind. so you shouldn't expect others to think that way also. it could also be a miracle for another person. maybe that bus stopped the car from plowing into a little old lady walking on the sidewalk. one could think its was a "miracle" that she wasnt hit. you see, anything and everything that happens in our world is just that, a HAPPENING. anything else is relative to the observer, but yet we try to have a "universal law" or "code" of what is good and bad and that just isnt fuckin correct. we shouldn't be allowed to do that, we arent GODS. just because we are at the top of the food chain with our technology doesnt mean we can be "judges"

of nature. sure we can think what we want, but you can
"think" and "believe" you can judge people and nature
all you want, but you are still wrong! why should
your morals apply to everyone else. "morals" is just
another word. and thats it. I think we are all a waste
of natural resources and should be killed off. and since
humans have the ability to choose... and I'm human...
I think I will choose to kill and damage as much
as nature allows me to. so take that. fuck you,
and eat napalm lead! HA! only nature can stop me.
I know I could get shot by a cop after only killing a single
person, but hey guess the fuck wHAT! I choose to kill
that one person so get over it! Its MY fault! not my
parents, not my brothers, not my friends, not my favorite
bands, Not computer games, not the media, IT is MINE!
so shut the fuck up!

             —REB—   7/29/98

someones bound to say "what were they thinking?" when we
go NBK or when we were planning it, so this is what I
am thinking. "I have a goal to destroy as much as possible
so I must not be sidetracked by my feelings of sympathy,
mercy, or any of that, so I will force myself to believe
that everyone is just another monster from Doom like FH
or FS or demons, so Its either me or them. I have to turn
off my feelings." keep this in mind, I want to burn the world,
I want to kill everyone except about 5 people, who I will
name later, so If you are reading this you are lucky you escaped
my rampage because I wanted to kill you. It will be very
tricky getting all of our supplies, explosives, weaponry, ammo, and
then hiding it all and then actually planting it all so we can
achieve our goal. but if we get busted any time, we start
killing then and there, just like Wilks from the AlIENS books,
I aint going out without a fight.

Once I finally start my killing, keep this in mind,
there are probalbly about 100 people max in the sthool alone
who I dont want to die, the rest, MUST FUCKING DIE! If I didn't
like you or if you pissed me off and lived through my attacks,
consider yourselfe one lucky god damn NIGGER. Pity that a lot of
the dead will be a waste in someways, like dead hot chicks who
were still bitches, they could have been good fucks. oh well,
too fucking bad. life isnt fair... not by a long fuckin shot when I'm
at the wheel, too. God I want to torch and level everything in this whole
fucking area but bombs of that size are hard to make, and plus I would
need a fuckin fully loaded A-10 to get every store on wadsworth and all the
buildings downtown. heh, imagine THAT ya fuckers, picture half of denver
on fire just from me and Vodka. ~~~~ napalm on sides of skyscrapers and
car-garages blowing up from exploded gas tanks.... oh man that would be
beautiful. ~ 10/23/98

You know what, I feel like teleing about lies, I lie a lot. almost
constant. and to everybody. just to keep my own ass out
of the water. and by the way (side note) I don't think I am doing
this for attention, as some people may think. Lets see,
what are some big lies I have told; "yeah I stopped smoking,"
"for doing it not for getting caught," "no I'm havent been making
more bombs," "no I wouldn't do that," and of course, countless of
other ones, and yeah I know that I hate liers and I am one
myself, oh fucking well. Its ok if I am a hypocrite, but
no one else, because I am higher then you people, no matter
what you say, if you disagree I would shoot you. And I am
one racist mother fucker too, fuck the niggers and spics
and chinks, unless they are cool, but sometimes they are
so fucking retarded they deserve to be ripped on. some people
go through life begging to be shot. and white fucks are just
the same. if I could nuke the world I would, because
so far I hate you all. there are porobly around 10 people
I wouldnt want to die, but hey, who ever said life is
fair should be shot like the others too. - 11/1/98

KKK

heh heh heh. I sure had fun this weekend. let's see, what really happened. before going to Rock n bowl we stopped by King Soopers and ▓▓▓ and ▓▓▓▓▓ picked up some big ass stogies. we then went to Rock n bowl and I had a few cigarettes and one of my brand new cigars. we then went back to ▓▓▓▓ house where her mom had previously bought us all a fuck load of liquor. personally I had asked for Tequilla and Irish cream, vodka got his vodka, and there was beer, whiskey, schnopps, puckers, scotch, and of course, orange juice! so we had some fun there playing cards and making drinks. we eventually made it to bed at about 5 AM. got up at 10, went to safeway got some donuts and then I took ▓▓ vodka home. the bottle of Tequilla is almost full and is in my car, right by my spare tire and right by the bottle of Irish cream. heh heh. I'll have to find a spot for those. and by the way, this napz report is boosting my love of killing even more. like the early nazi government, my brain is like a sponge, sucking up everything that sounds cool and leaving out all that is worthless, that's how Nazism was formed, and that's how I will be too! 11/8/98

Fuck you Brady! all I want is a couple of guns, and thanks to your fucking bill I will probalby not get any! come on, I'll have a clean record and I only want them for personal protection. It's not like I'm some psycho who would go on a shooting spree..... fuckers. I'll probally end up nuking everything and fucking robbing some gun collectors house. Fuck, that'll be hard. oh well, just as long as I kill a lot of fucking people. Everyone is always making fun of me because of how I look, how fucking weak I am and shit, well I will get you all back: ultimate fucking revenge here. you people could have shown more respect, treated me better, asked for my knowledge or guidance more, treated me more like a senior, and maybe I wouldn't have been so ready to tear your fucking heads off. then again, I have always hated how I looked, I make fun of people who look like me, sometimes without even thinking sometimes just because I want to rip on myself. that's where a lot of my hate grows from, the fact that I have practically no self esteem, especially concerning girls and looks and such. therefore people make fun of me ... constantly... therefore I get no respect and therefore I get fucking PISSED. as of this date I have enough explosives to kill about 100 people, and then if I get a couple bayonetts, swords, axes, wtc I'll be able to kill at least 10 more. and that just isn't enough!

17

Guns! I _need_ guns! Give me some fucking firearms!
11/12/98

HATE! I'm full of hate and I Love it. I HATE PEOPLE. and they
better fucking fear me if they know whats good for em. yes I hate and I guess
I want others to know it, yes I'm racist and I don't mind. Niggs and spics bring
it on to themselves, and another thing, I am very racist towards white trash p.o.s.s like
███████ and ████ they deserve the hatred, otherwise I probly wouldn't hate them.
Its a tragedy, the human nature of people will lead to their downfall. Peoples human
nature will get them killed. whether by me or Vodka, Its happened before, and not
just in school shootings like those pussy dumbasses over in Minnesota who squeeled.
throughout history, Its our fucking nature! I know how people are and why
and I cant stand it! I love the nazis too... by the way, I fucking cant get
enough of the swastika, the SS, and the iron cross. Hitler and his head
boys fucked up a few times and it cost them the war, but I love their beliefs and
who they were, what they did, and what they wanted. I know that form of gov
couldn't have lasted long once the human equation was brought in, but dammit
it sure looked good. every form of gov. leads to downfalls, everything will
always fuck up or yeah something, its all Doomed god dammit. this is beginning
to make me get in a corner. I'm showing too much of myself, my views and
thoughts, people might start to wonder, smart ones will get nosey and something
might happen to fuck me over, I might need to put on one helluva mask here
to fool you all some more. fuck fuck fuck it'll be very fucking hard to hold
out until April. If people would give me more compliments all of this might
still be avoidable... but probably not. whatever I do people make fun of
me, and sometimes directly to my face. I'll get revenge soon enough. fuckers
shouldn't have ripped on me so much huh! HA! then again its human nature to
do what you did... so I guess I am also attacking the human race. I cant take it,
its not right... true... correct... perfect. I fucking hate the human equation.
Nazism would be fucking great if it werent for individualism and our natural instinct
to aske questions. you know what maybe I just need to get laid. maybe
that'll just change some shit around. thats another thing, I am a fucking
dog. I have fantasies of just taking someone and fucking them hard
and strong. someone like ████████ were I just ████ pick her up,
take her to my room, tear off her shirt and pants and just eat her
out and fuck her hard. I love flesh... weisses fleisch! dein weisses fleisch
erregt mich so... Ich bin doch nur ein Gigilo! I want to grab a few different
girls in my gym class, take them into a room, pull their pants off and fuck
them hard. I love flesh... the smooth legs, the large breasts, the ████ innocent
flawless body, the eyes, the hair; jet black, blond, white, brown, ahhh I just
want to fuck! call it teenage hormones or call it a crazy fuckin racist rapist... ☺ its nur egal

18

I just want to be surrounded by the flesh of a woman, someone like ██████ who I wanted to just fuck like hell, she made me practically drool, when she wore those shorts to work... instant hard on. ~ I couldn't stop staring. and others like ██████ in my gym class, ██████ or whatever in my gym class, and others who I just want to overpower and engulf myself in them. mmmm I can taste the sweet flesh now... the salty sweet, the animalistic movement... feechhh... lieaebe... ..... fleisccchhhh... who can I trick into my room first? I can sweep someone off their feet, tell them what they want to hear, be all nice and sweet, and then "fuck em like an animal, feel them from the inside" as Reznor said. oh ~ that's something else... that one NIN video I saw, broken or closer or something, the one where the guy is kidnapped and tortured like hell... actual hell. I want to do that too. I want to tear a throat out with my own teeth like a pop can. I want to gut someone with my hand, to tear a head off and rip out the heart and lungs from the neck, to stab someone in the gut, shove it up to the heart, and yank the fucking blade out of their rib cage! I want to grab some weak little freshman and just tear them apart like a fucking wolf. show them who is god. strangle them, squish their head, bite their temples into the skull, rip off their jaw. rip off their collar bones, break their arms in half and twist them around, the lovely sounds of bones cracking and flesh ripping, ahh... so much to do and so little chances. ~ 11/17/98

"weisses Fleisch"
- perfect
- song
- for
- me.

Well folks, today was a very important day in the history of R. Today, along with Vodka and someone else who I wont name, we went downtown and purchased the following; a double barrel 12ga. shotgun, a pump action 12ga. shotgun, a 9mm carbine, 250 9mm rounds, 15 12ga slugs, 40 shotgun shells, 2 switch blade knives, and a total of 4·10 round clips for the carbine. we....... have........ GUNS! we fucking got em you sons of bitches! HA!! HAHAHA! neener! Booga Booga. heh. its all over now, this capped it off, the point

of no return, I have my carbine, shotgun, ammo and knife all in my trunk tonight, and they'll stay there till tomorrow... after school you know, its really a shame. I had a lot of fun at that gun show, I would have loved it if you were there dad. we would have done some major bonding. would have been great, oh well. but, alas, I fucked up and told ██ about my "flask" that really disappoints me ██ I know you thought it was good for me in the long run and all that shit, smart of you to give me such a big raise and then cut me out, you figure it was supposed to cancel each other? god damn flask, that just fucked me over bigtime. now you all will be on my ass even more than before about being on track. I'll get around it though. I'll have to cheat and lie to everyone then thats fine. THIS is what I am motivated for. THIS = my goal. THIS is what I want "to do with my life". you know whats weird, I dont feel like punching through a door because of the flask deal, probly cause

19

I am fucking armed ~~now~~. I feel more confident, stronger, more God-like. I have confidence in my ability to deceive people. hopefully I'll make it to April, but that might not happen. ug, Its been a busy weekend, I need to sleep, I'll continue ~~tomorrow~~ tomorrow.

11/22/98

yesterday we fired our first actual firearms ever. 3 rounds from the carbine. taught ~~that~~ ground a thing or 2. I even had the 2 clips in my pocket while talking to vodkas dad about senior ditch day, God it felt great firing off that bad boy, and hopefully I'll be able to get more than just 4 clips for it. I dubbed my shotgun "Arlene" after Arlene Sanders from the Doom books. she always did love the shotgun. vodka's DB is looking very fucking awesome, all cut down to the proper lengths. This is a bitch trying to keep up on homework while working on my guns, bombs, and lying. ~~as~~ by the way, I bought that flask in the mall and I had a friend fill it up w/ scotch whiskey, only had about 3 swigs in the 3 weeks I had it. plus monday I gave my T and IC to Vodka, just in case. I never really did like alcohol, just wasn't my thing, but It felt good to ~~just~~ have around. That arguement on the 22nd was a real bitch, but I think I should have won a fucking oscar. I even quoted a few movies, remember "what the hell am I gonna do now man?! what am I gonna do!?" thats good ole Hudson from aliens. sounded good too. and hey goddamnit I would have been a fucking great marine, It would have given me a reason to do good. and I would never drink and drive, either. It will be weird when we actually go on the rampage. hopefully we will have plenty of clips and bombs. I'm gonna still try and get my calico 9mm. just think, 100 rounds without reloading.... hell yeah!

we actually may have a chance to get some machine pistols thanks to the Brady bill. if we can save up about 200$ real quick ~~and~~ and find someone who is 21+ we can go to the next gun show and find a private dealer and buy ourselves some bad ass AB-10 machine pistols. Clips for those things can get really fucking big too.

12/3/98

Woohoo, I'll never have to ~~take~~ a final again! feels good to be free. I just love Hobbes and Nietzche. Well tomorrow I'll be ordering 9 more 10 round clips for my carbine. I'm gonna be so fucking loaded in about a month. the big things we need to figure out now is the time bombs for the commons and how we will get them in ~~the~~ and leave them there to go off, without any fuckin Jews finding them. I wonder if anyone will wright a book on me. sure is a Ton of symbolism, double meanings, themes, appearence vs reality shit going on here. oh well, it better be fuckin good if it is wrttin.

12/17/98

i just got this. KMFDM's new album is entitled "Adios" and its release date is in April. how fuckin appropriate, a subliminal final "Adios" tribute to Reb and vodka, thanks KMFDM... I ripped the hell onto the system.

12/20/98

jeeus christ that was fucking close. fucking shitheads at the gun shop almost dropped the whole project. oh well, thank god I can BS so fucking well. I went and picked up those babies today, so now I got 13 of those niggers WOOHAH. the stereo is very nice, but having no insurance payments to worry about so I could concentrate of BOMBS would have been better. oh well, I think I'll have enough. now I just need to get Vodka another gun.

12/29/98

Months have passed. Its the first Friday night in the final month. much shit has happened. Vodka has a Tec 9, we test fired all of our babies, we have 6 time clocks ready, ▓▓▓ 39 crickets, 24 pipe Bombs, and the napalm is under construction. Right now I'm trying to get fucked and trying to finish off these time bombs NBK came quick. why the fuck can't I get any? I mean, I'm nice and considerate and all that shit, but nooooo. I think I try to hard. but I kinda need to considering NBK is closing in. The amount of dramatic isony and foreshadowing is fucking amazing. Everything I see and hear I incorporate into NBK somehow. Either bombs, clocks, guns, napalm, killing people, any and everything finds some tie to it. feels like a Goddamn movie sometimes. I wanna try to put some mines and trip bombs around this town too maybe. Get a few extra frags on the scoreboard. I hate you people for leaving me out of so many fun things. And no don't fucking say "well thats your fault" because it isnt, you people had my phone#, and I asked and all, but no. no no no don't let the wierd looking Eric KID come along, ooh fucking nooo.

4/3/99

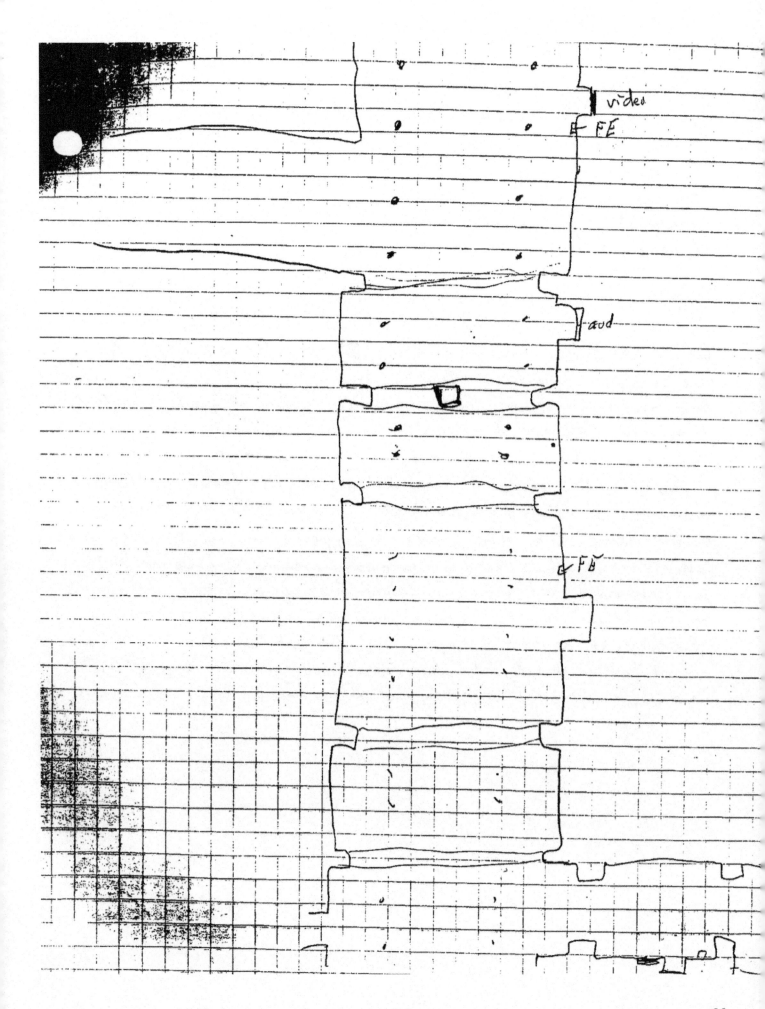

video

FE

aud

FE

22

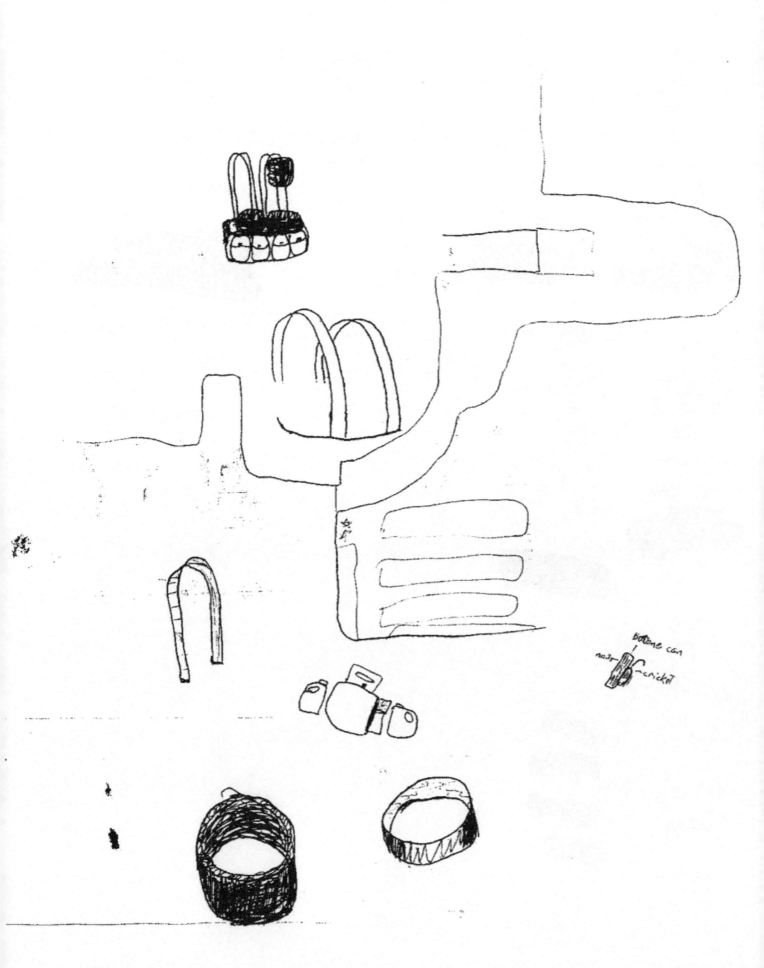

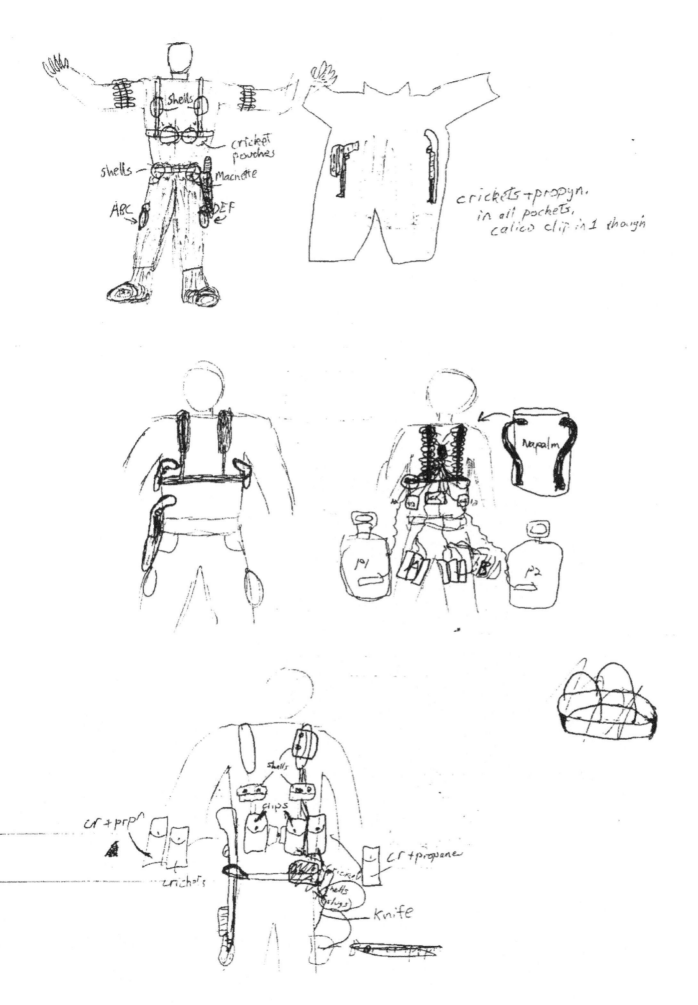

crickets + propyn.
in all pockets,
calico clip in 1 though

shells
cricket pouches
shells
Machette
ABC
DEF

Napalm
P1
P2

cr + prpn
crichets
shells
clips
cr + propane
shells slugs
knife

25

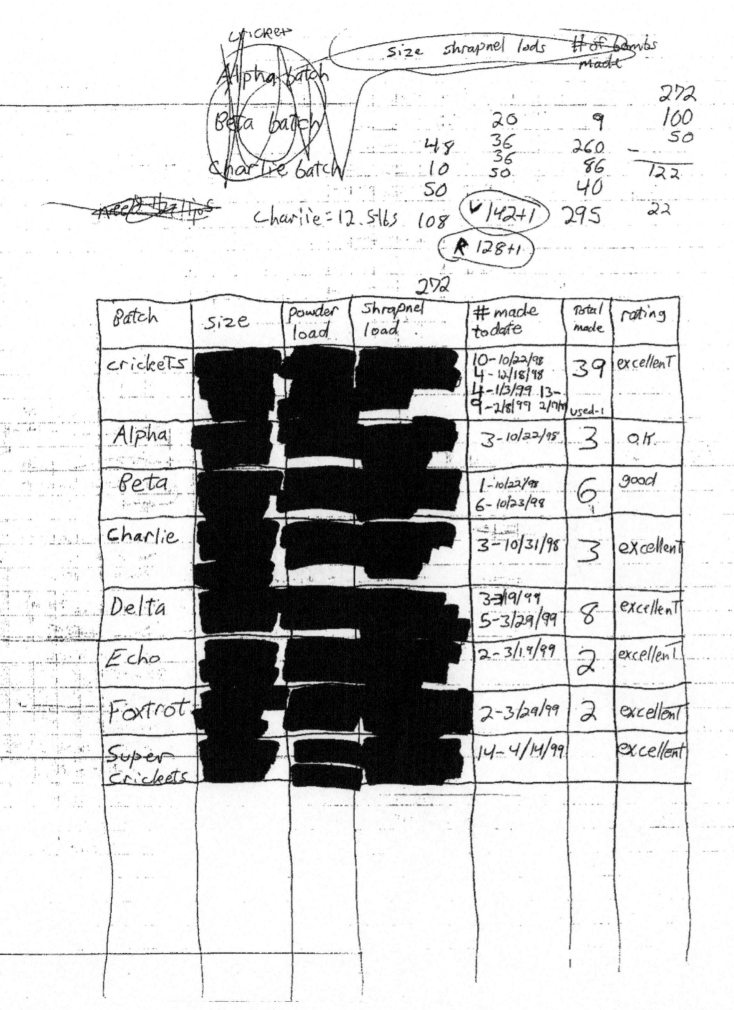

cricket

	Size	shrapnel lods	# of bombs made
Alpha batch			272
Beta batch	20	9	100
	48	36	260 — 50
Charlie batch	10	36	86 — 122
	50	50	40

need tails

Charlie = 12.5 lbs   108   ✓ 142 + 1   295   22

R 128 + 1

272

Batch	size	powder load	shrapnel load	# made to date	Total made	rating
crickets	███	███	███	10 – 10/22/98 4 – 12/18/98 4 – 1/3/99 13 – 9 – 2/8/99 2/17/99 used-1	39	excellent
Alpha	███	███	███	3 – 10/22/98	3	O.K.
Beta	███	███	███	1 – 10/22/98 6 – 10/23/98	6	good
Charlie	███	███	███	3 – 10/31/98	3	excellent
Delta	███	███	███	3 – 3/9/99 5 – 3/29/99	8	excellent
Echo	███	███	███	2 – 3/19/99	2	excellent
Foxtrot	███	███	███	2 – 3/29/99	2	excellent
Super crickets	███	███	███	14 – 4/14/99		excellent

Have　　　　　Need

$ ~~300~~

200 money
order
wise

#200 ~~45 CDs~~

~~$200 – 4-6 mnths~~

300 – at 3/26

↑
200 – at 4/9

↑
BD $?

~~$300 – ammunition + clips~~

~~$200 – ~~

~~$90 – shells~~

~~$200 – holster, carrying strings~~

~~$—~~

$ 20 – Gasoline

~~$—~~

$200 + – Explosives (Propane tanks, camping fuel tanks, etc)

~~A B+ 9 + 14 3 clips – holster~~

~~(machine pistol)~~

~~· suspenders~~

150-R +2s

$ 50 per tank

shit left
to do at 3/22/99

~~✳ figure out napolm
recipe + storage
area.~~

– ~~time schedule~~
~~the commons/~~
~~people patterns~~

– 9mm ammo (150-200)

– ~~shells (50)~~

– practice in-car
gear up

~~– lasers for carbine~~

– get laid ✗

– prepare explosives
↳ distractions
↳ commons
↳ cars
↳ grenades

~~Boat~~　~~powder~~　~~rifle~~

~~Shotgun~~　~~Shells~~　~~Assault weapon~~

Explosives　~~Bullets~~　Time Bombs

560

shotgun
36 shells + 5 loaded
carbine
~~12~~ clips + 1 loaded
switchblade
boot knife
long knife

230 – propane　(4) + refill
25 – 9mm ammo (100)
~~25 – 00 Buck (30)~~
15 – Gas　(10-13 gal?)
~~30 – lasers (2)~~

39?

27

Cannon Fuse

Napalm Tests:

— shitty but in a fix would do ok

good burning. very slick.

worthless

needs to be heated, no time

worthless

ok. needs more expirements (need to allow it to soak it and dissolve)

worthless

good but need larger testing + boil

heated ? no time

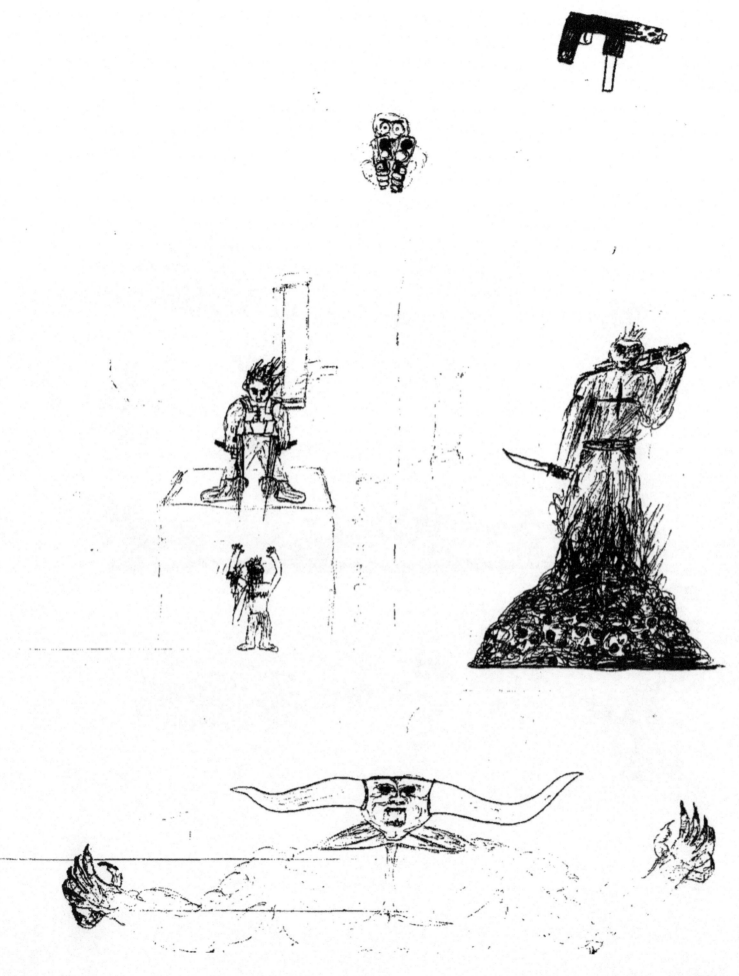

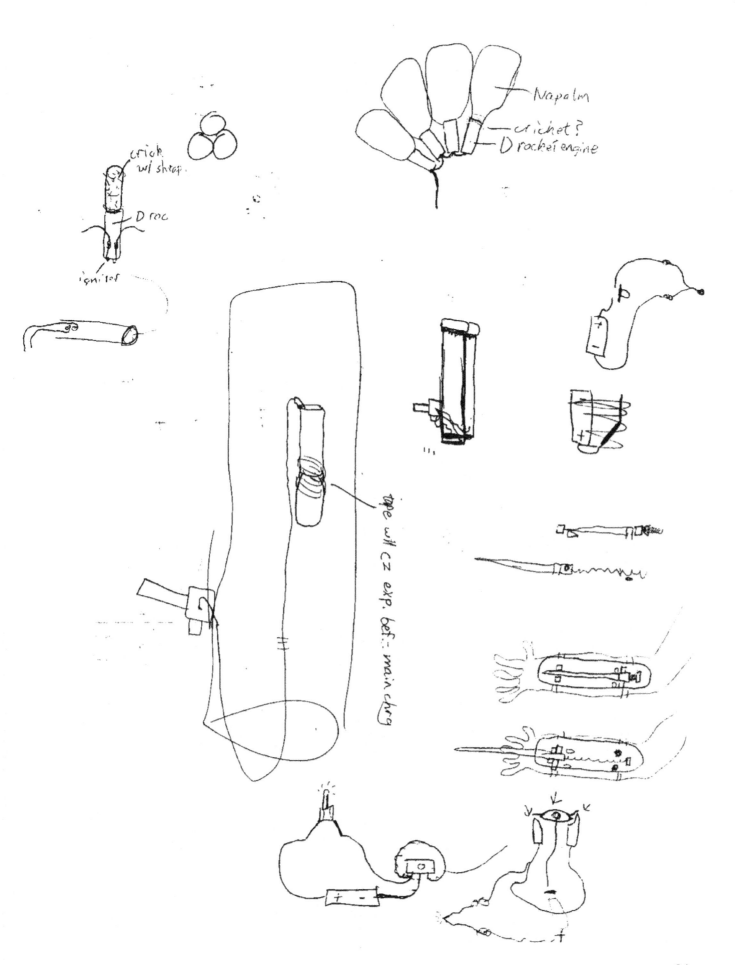

crick
w/ shap.

D roc

ignitor

Napalm

cricket?
D rocket engine

tape will cz exp. bef. main chrg

31

BUNKER: whiskey

4 MGs (mortar grenades)
1 Cricket (black)
3 (Alpha Batch)
+ 10 crickets
─────────────────
18 explosives

NOTECARD BOX
29 crickets

Website

YOU KNOW WHAT I HATE!!!?

---SLOW PEOPLE!! You know those people who walk like a lifeguard on baywatch runs! Slow as molasses! MOVE IT OR LOOSE IT PUNKS!

YOU KNOW WHAT I HATE!!!?

---When there is a group of trendy punk like little smart asses standing in the middle of a hallway or walkway, and they are just STANDING there talking and blocking my way!!! Bloody snotty people think they are god almighty and can just stop and talk away wherever or whenever they please, learn some manners you stuck up people!!

YOU KNOW WHAT I HATE!!!?

---When people dont watch where THEY ARE GOING! Then they plow into me and say "oops, sorry." or "watch it!" NNNYAAAA!!! Like it couldnt possibly be their fault that we collided. Oh, heaven forbid your holy graciousness being the cause of something baaaaad.....RRRRRR!!!!

YOU KNOW WHAT I LOVE!!!?

---When some rich stuck up piece of s!@# white trash person gets in a car wreck with their brand new car!

YOU KNOW WHAT I LOVE!!!?

---When some stupid retarded kid blows his damn hand off because he couldnt figure out that a lit fuse means that the firecracker is going to go off soon! HAHAHA!!

YOU KNOW WHAT I HATE!!!?

---OOOOOOOJAAAAAAAAAAAAY!!!!!!!!!! GOD I F-ING HATE THAT WORTHLESS TRIAL!!! Who in their right feeeeearrrRIGIN mind would care about that trial??!? its not any different from any other murder trial! Tell those worthless reporters to get a life! And what the hell do we have to gain by watching that stupid trial anyay!!? Its not news! its a trial! not news! trail! Trialdoes not = news!

YOU KNOW WHAT ELSE I HATE!!!?

---Jon binay however the flip you spell her spoiled name Ramsee!!!! We dont care! Good flipping riddens!!! What the flame do you expect if you flicking put your kid in all these beauty pagents when shes 4 years old!! Makes her look like a SLUUUUUUUUUUUT!!!!!!

YOU KNOW WHAT I HATE!!!?

---STUPID PEOPLE!!! Why must so many people be so stupid!!?

YOU KNOW WHAT I LOVE!!!?

---Making fun of stupid people doing stupid things! Like one time when i was watching this freshman try to get on a computer that needed a password....he typed in the password.......and waited. The retard didnt press enter or any thing. He just waited. Then he started cussing at the computer saying it was screwed up. Then the freshman went and got a teacher and the flippin teacher could not figure out why it wasnt going anywhere!!! JESUS!! Personaly i think they should be smacked across the face a couple million times er so.....give or take 1.

YOU KNOW WHAT I LOVE!!!?

---Natural SELECTION!!!!!!!!!! God damn its the best thing that ever happened to the Earth. Getting rid of all the stupid and weak organisms......but its all natural!! YES! I wish the government would just take off every warning label. So then all the dumbasses would either severely hurt themselves or DIE! And boom, no more dumbasses. heh.

YOU KNOW WHAT I HATE!!!?

---RUDE PEOPLE THAT CUT!!!!! Why the flip cant you wait like every other human on earth does. If you cut, you are the following: Stuck up, self centered, selfish, lazy, impatient, rude, and.....damn i ran out of adjectives. anyway. Every flippin line i get into i end up having to wait a flaming hour when there WAS only me and 1 other person in the line! Then the asshole lets all his\her so called friends cut in behind em!

YOU KNOW WHAT I REALLY HATE!!!?

---LIARS!!! OH GAWWWWWD I HATE LIARS. And living in this neighborhood there is thousands of them!!! Why the flip must people lie so damn much! Especially about stupid things! Like "Yeah, i just bought 5 cases of M-80's in Oklahoma for about $5. And they are legal there and everything. Yeah my parents buy most of my guns, every once in a while ill use my 4,000 dollar paycheck and buy a shotgun or 2. And my brand new hummer just broke down on the highway when i was going 250mph. Stupid cars." like that. now. what flaming part if any would a normal human being believe? And thats just one person!! Another BIG example is Brooks Brown(303-972-0602). Now, according to him, he has a 215 IQ, 5 other homes (2 in alaska, and 3 in Florida), 95mph fast ball(he is only 16), runs a mile in about 5 minutes, has an uncle thats the former head of all the armed forces and has access to.....Theee Button..., his other uncle is a multi-millionare that lives in downtown detroit, and his neighbors are the chick that sang "r.e.s.p.e.c.t." and the lead singer of Aerosmith. And that same uncle owns 30%

of the stock of that tylenol company, And his grandparents gives..GIVES...him about 1000 dollars for each month, and his other Grandpa can blow up every house in America because all the houses have C-4 in the foundations. Again, according to Brook Brown. OK, when people lie like that, its not impressive, noone believes it, it sounds just plain stupid, and its a friggin waste of my time.

YOU KNOW WHAT I HATE!!!?

—R rated movies on CABLE! My DOG can do a better damn editing job than those tards!!! For the sake of all television they can at least try to make it sound like actual words the person would say! If you have ever seen Aliens or Predator you'll know what I'm talking about.

YOU KNOW WHAT I HATE!!!?

—Windows Keys!!!!

YOU KNOW WHAT I LOVE!!!?

—WAREZ!!! Why pay when its free?

YOU KNOW WHAT I HATE!!!?

---People who think they can forecast the weather!!! Then they think that everyone else will think that they are cool just because you said that we were gonna have a 4 foot blizzard starting today! Like just the other day, this punk i know was saying.."Yeah tomorrow we are gonna get like, 2 feet of snow in just a few hours, They were saying its gonna be the biggest snow in ten years. Yeah. Itll be about -60 outside too." And that day we get an inch of snow and its 26 out.

YOU KNOW WHAT I HATE!!!?

---Cuuuuuuuuhntryyyyyyyyy music!!!

YOU KNOW WHAT I LOVE!!!?

---Zippo Lighters!!!!!

YOU KNOW WHAT I HATE!!!?

—People who say that wrestling is real!! now, im talking about the matches like hulk hogan or undertaker. If you think that these matches arent faked and that these guys are REALLY punching and breaking arms, then please mail me. I would love to know where you live so i can BOMB your fucking house and ACTUALLY BREAK YOUR ARMS!☺

YOU KNOW WHAT I HATE!!!?

—YOUNG SMOKERS! they think they are so god damn cool with their big bad ciggarettes and their "sooo cool" attitude. I cant wait until they are about 25 and have to breathe through their friggin necks and talk with a computer hooked up to their formal-vocal cords.

YOU KNOW WHAT I HATE!!!?

---PAYING FOR MY CAR INSURANCE!!!

YOU KNOW WHAT I LOVE!!!?

—FREEDOM OF SPEEEECH!!!

YOU KNOW WHAT I HATE!!!?

---Freedom of the press. I hate that part of the Bill of Rights.

YOU KNOW WHAT I HATE!!!?

—People who are against the death penalty!!! i think the courts should flaming fry every convicted felon out there!

YOU KNOW WHAT I LOVE!!!?

—SCHOOL!

YOU KNOW WHAT I HATE!!!?

---SCHOOLWORK!

YOU KNOW WHAT I REALLY HATE!!!?

---COMMERCIALS!!! OH GAWWD I HATE COMMERCIALS!!! The only ones i MIGHT like are previews and some car commercials. But jesus christ, all those Lotion, PERFUME, Makeup, JCPENNYS, Joslins, food, coffee, or advertisement commercials! Please! Destroy them all! never record another! They suck! They are only funny the first time! Think up other stuff! They suck! They are stupid! We get sick of them VERY FAST! VERY! VERY FAST!

YOU KNOW WHAT I HATE!!!!?

---TRENDS!!! I HATE trends! Like tommy hilfiger or mossimo or SKA or those little chapstick lip gloss lip cream CRAP that every freakin girl in middle and high school carries around! They are just so......DAMN......rrr.....RR... ANNOYING!!!! YAA'AH!!! RRRRR!!!!

YOU KNOW WHAT I HATE!!!?

---People who dont believe in personal hygiene. For the love of god. and for the sake of god, CLEAN UP! Frickin people with 2 inch fingernails and a whole frickin flower pot full of dirt under them and raggy hair or shirts stained to hell. Or people that just plain stink, and they dont do anything about it. Now, im not making fun of anyone if they cant help it, or afford it or anything like that, thats not their fault, but if your some kid drivin a ford explorer and have yellow teeth, then thats just plain unhuman.

YOU KNOW WHAT I HATE!!!?

---People who use the same word over and over again! Like, "actually", or "shazame", or "nifty". Read a fuckin book or two, increase your vo-cab-u-lary ya f*ck*ng idiots.

YOU KNOW WHAT I HATE!!!?

---People who try to impress me by TRYING to brag about the militaries weapons! Now, to some of you this might seem, wierd, but its happened. Like this, "dude, they just came out with this new chemical that can destroy denver only using a cubic inch of it. The military is keeping it all locked up because if it gets to close to water it explode, and the force would create a cresent earth, maaan." Yeah, right, bullshit, or like this, "Dude, the air force has tracked santa clause for like, 10 years now, he is real man. its all a cover up." or "The air force just made a plane that can bend light man, its completely invisible." now, this is just some of the shit i've heard. it makes me SICK. And they arent even in the frickin military nor do they know anyone that is even if it WAS true and like they would know about it! GAWD!! I HATE those PEOPLE!

YOU KNOW WHAT ELSE I HATE!!!?

---People who THINK they are martial arts experts! They are all cocky and thinkin that they are all big and bad. saying bullshit like, "yeah if you snap your fingers right here the sound waves will melt the brain and youll die from your own brain poring out your ears." or "if you flick someone right here their arteries will burst and they will drown in their own blood." freakin hate it when they keep sayin "your own", like it would be someone elses!?!? then when these shitheads get in real fights the get their frickin asses wooped all over the place by some little girl.

YOU KNOW WHAT I HATE!!!?

---STAR WARS FANS!!! GET A FaaaaaaRIGIN LIFE YOU BORING GEEEEEKS!

YOU KNOW WHAT I HATE!!!?

---RACISM!!! Anyone who hate blacks, asians, mexicans, or people from any other country or race just because they arent from here or are a different color...woopie freakin doo man. And that goes for black people too. I've seen people on Ricki Lake or Opra or whatever saying things like "white boy, whitie, you say dat cuz you be white, yea..you white people all du same, she be white, so she baaad, I bet he did dat stuff cuz he a white boy" allll that stuff just pisses me off to no end. It is possible for BLACKS to be RACIST too ya KNOW.....people who think that should be drug out into the street, have their arms ripped off, be burnt shut at the stumps, then have every person of the race that YOU hate come out and beat the crap out of you. You people are the scum of society and arent worth a damn piece of worm crap. You all are trash. And dont let me catch you making fun of someone just because they are a different color because i will come in and break your f*ck*ng legs with a plastic spoon. i dont care how long it takes! and thats both legs mind you.

YOU KNOW WHAT I HATE!!!?

---THOSE FREAKIN ADVERTISING OR CHARITY CALLS! People saying "Hi, im not selling anything but"----good, now shut the flip up and go get a real job!---well! you are so rude!"---damn strait and if you dont get off my line ill come down to your building and shove that phone list up your arse and take the phone and shove it up your boss's arse! "click" heeeheeee, that would be cool.

YOU KNOW WHAT I HATE!!!?

---When people mispronounce words! and they dont even know it to. like acrosT, or eXspreso, pacific (specific), or 2 pAck. learn to speak correctly you morons.

YOU KNOW WHAT I HATE!!!?

When people drive really slow in the fast lane!!! GOD!!! Those people do NOT...NOT..NOT..NOT know how to drive!! Anyone who knows anything about driving knows that if you are passing someone or going really really really fast, you should stay in the slow lane!! Anyone caught doing that should be sent to every driving class available for a flaming year!

YOU KNOW WHAT I HATE!!!?

THE "W.B." network!!!! OH JESUS MARY MOTHER OF GOD ALMIGHTY I HATE THAT CHANNEL WITH ALL MY HEART AND SOUL. Their stupid "dubba dubba hey dubba hoe dubba B dubba boo dubba foo dubba dubba wubba lubba HEY dubba hoe dubba" CRAP!! Are they purposely doing that just to piss me off!!!??? JESUUUUS!!!

YOU KNOW WHAT I HATE!!!?
Basketball!
YOU KNOW WHAT I HATE!!!?
PUFFY DADDY OR PUFFY COMBS OR PUFFY SMALLS OR WHATEVER THE HELL HIS NAME IS!! I hate that guy!!!!! Why doesnt anyone "bust a cap" in his ass??? He cant even rap worth a damn! All his songs are like "mmm yeah huh Uu Uu Uu yeyah mgmmmmbmm yeeeeyahh jjjjeya Uoo UU uu…..mmmtmdlkg mmmmmmmtgmmmm yaaahhh…. Uu…" and stuff. I HATE THAT GUY!!!
YOU KNOW WHAT I HATE!!!?
PEOPLE WHO ARE MEAN TO ANIMALS!!!!! The only promise I make in this whole page is this: if I ever see anyone on god's green earth harm a dog or be mean or unkind to any mammal, I will SEVERELY hurt you, I swear to god, I swear on my computer, on my car, on my fucking LIFE I will hurt you.
YOU KNOW WHAT I LOVE!!!?
Driving FAST!!
YOU KNOW WHAT I HATE!!!?
SKA!
YOU KNOW WHAT I LOVE!!!?
Good, fast, hard, strong, pounding TECHNO!! Such as KMFDM, PRODIGY, ORBITAL, RAMMSTEIN, and such.
YOU KNOW WHAT I HATE!!!?
RAPPERS AND THEIR OH SO SMOOTH COOL SUAVE RAPPER ATTITUDE!!!!!
YOU KNOW WHAT I HATE!!!?
RAP VIDEOS!!! Every geeeawd damn one of them is the same! 5 chicks all with color coordinated outfits and little nylon jackets and spandex pants dancing around while some dorky rapper moans and groan around and drives a fancy car and waves his arms around acting like a freakin DORK!
YOU KNOW WHAT I HATE!!!?
HOMOSEXUALS!! It is just plain WRONG.
People who tell me what I think or what I do or what I should say! Sometimes its ok, like if its a psychiatrist or something, but if its just some other "dude" at school telling me I shouldn't think something or some teacher telling me I cant go down some hallway, then I say FUCK YOU I do what ever the figgide flame I want!!
YOU KNOW WHAT I HATE!!!?
G rated MOVIES!! Like the Lion King or HERCULES or Warriors of Virtue. I don't care who they are made for I DON'T LIKE THEM!
YOU KNOW WHAT I LOVE!!!?
FREEDOM!
YOU KNOW WHAT I HATE!!!?
U.S.A.'s La femme Nikita. Stupidest damn show I have ever seen. Little swat team navy seals wanna be dorks.
YOU KNOW WHAT I LOVE!!!?
PUNCHING THINGS!
YOU KNOW WHAT I HATE!!!?
HANSON! Little pansy ass WUSSES!! Girls like them cause they think they're boys and Boys like them cause they think they're GIRLS!!
YOU KNOW WHAT I HATE!!!?
IRAQ!! Nuke em all!!
YOU KNOW WHAT I LOVE!!!?
When I catch someone doing something that i told em not too do! Then im just like….now now, how should I kick your ass…hmmm.

Freshman!!! They are freakin everywhere and they are pissin me the hell off!

Religions!!! Jesus is dead...get over it!!! the bible is just a freakin BOOK!! I would sooner burn to death than say I worship some egotistical god!!

Retards!!! They are a waste of time and money and effort and energy and space and lots of other stuff too! They need to DIE!!

Puff freakin daddy!!! He sucks! He can absolutely NOT rap!!! No one can, because rap is GAY

Missy elliot!! Stupid fat ugly barrel of LARD!

Lil kim!!! Another stupid fat ugly barrel of LARD!!

Mace!! Another wannabe star who THINKS he can rap but really CAAANT!

Masta P another rapper! Too many rappers!!!

will smith!! God damn did he ever sell out!! He was cool, but then he started doing these videos again!

RAP VIDEOS!! They are all the same!! 5 stupid cheerleaders in color coordinated nylon outfits dancing around infront of a curved orblike camera with a dumbass guy walkin around swingin his arms sayin "uh huh yeyah werd up you know what im sayin uh huh mmmmhm yeya babey"

hanson!!! Stupid little possers who think they are cool! I still think atleast one of them is a girl!!

GAP! God damn trends!! Why are they sooo original!! If its made in a factory its not very freakin original!!

TOMMY HILFIGER!! They remind of the nazis by how that damn hilfiger name is all over the place just like the swastika! Think about that one!!

OLD NAVY!! What the hell is wrong with those commercials?? Are they supposed to be that stupid??!

AMBERCROMBE and futch!!! Yet another yuppie dumbass wannabe trend!!

edie bower!! More trends!!

SKA!! People who like SKA give the rest of the human race a bad name!! They think they are soooo cool with their pot and flowers and condom hats and big baggy pants and wallet chains and sandals and CRAP!!

skatelites

five iron frenzy

skanking

dancing!! Have you ever looked at people dancing and seen how uterly stuupid they look!! Doesnt that give you a clue about yourself dancing!!

less than jake

pie tasters

bills dog verne!! First of all the name itself is retarded, and second of all the band SUCKS!!

real big fish

aquabats

blink 182

311

cops! Stupid law enforcing people!!!

LOVE----beef jerky!!

Politics!!

Clinton jokes!! For gods sake the joke is over so just shut up about him!!!

Foreigners!! Get out of my country!! Or atleast learn english and take a few driving classes!!!

American furniture warehouse!! With their stupid commercials with that freakin annoying old man and his uglyass daughter and his uglier ass granddaughter and all those god damn wild animals crawlin around on their furniture!!!

It would be great if god removed all vaccines and warning lables from everything in the world and let natural selection take its course. All the fat ugly retarded crippled dumbass stupid fuckheads in the world would die, and oh fucking well if a few of the good guys die to. Maybe then the human race can actually be proud of itself. World war II is the last time I bet America was proud of its self. We beat the fuck out of the damn zipperheads and the nazis. We came back, from being bombed and loosing major battles to nuke that little piece of shit island and to take over that cool place called Deustchland. I say its cool because I love the German language and "BRUTE" stuff. Kein mitleid fur die merheit. Put everyone in doom I and see who can get past atleast level 1. Actually, then put them into MY worlds. Like Thrasher, Whiskey, UAC Labs, und TIER. I would love to see all you fuckheads die. NBK. I love it! sometime in april me and V will get revenge and will kick natural selection up a few notches. Armed with the following; a terroist bag full of noisey crickets, noisey crickets strapped to WD40 cans, pipe bombs with a shit load of shrapnel, fire bombs, chlorine gas bombs, and smoke bombs. Fire arms we arent sure of yet, hopefully V will have his #3 and plenty of ammo for it. thats another thing, ill fuck around with some shotgun shells for more bombs also. For me, I don't know what weapon ill have. I just want a firearm that can hold lots of bullets and that wont jam on me. So ill need lots of clips to. Ill have those strapped onto my chest. Maybe a bullet proof vest too. We will be in all black. Dusters, black army pants, and we will get custom shirts that say R or V in the background in one big letter and NBK in the front in a smaller font. We will have knifes and blades and backup weaponry all over our bodies, I will have a tattoo of REB on my right arm. Once we start we will wear balaclavas. First we will go to the house of ██ and ████ in the morning before school starts and before anyone is even awake. We go in, we silently kill each inhabitant and then pin down ████ an ███ Then take our sweet time pissing on them, spitting on them, and just torturing the hell out of them. Once we are done there we set time bombs to burn the houses down and take any weaponry that we find, who knows we may get lucky. Then get totally prepared and during Alunch we go in and park in our spots. With sunglasses on we start carrying in all of our bags of terrorism and anarchism shit into our table. Being very casual and silent about it. its all for a science/band/english project or something. Then, we sit down, play some pumpup music, light a 50$ stoge, and get ready to start throwing out the first wave of crickets. Then, we light them, and throw them as far as we can, once the first wave starts to go off and the chaos begins, V opens fire and I start lobin the firebombs. Then I open fire and V starts lobin more crickets. Then if we can we go upstairs and go to each classroom we can and pick off fuckers at our will. If we still can we will hijack some awesome car, and drive off to the neighborhood of our choice and start torching houses with molotov cocktails. by that time cops will be all over us and we start to kill them to!we use bombs, fire bombs, and anything we fucking can to kill and damage as much as we fucking can. if it comes to the time when we are trapped with absolutely no way out, we eat crickets along with a ton of chlorine or some other deadly gas. so when we die, so will anyone close to us. if we have figured out the art of time bombs before hand, we will set hundreds of them around houses, roads, bridges, buildings and gas stations. anything that will cause damage and chaos. if you have ever seen the first few c

lips of violence in INVASION USA youll know what im talkin about. itll be like the LA riots, the oklahoma bombing, WWII, vietnam, duke and doom all mixed together. maybe we will even start a little rebelion or revolution to fuck things up as much as we can. i want to leave a lasting impression on the world. and god damnit do not blame anyone else besides me and V for this. dont blame my family, they had no clue and there is nothing they could have done, they brought me up just fucking fine, dont blame toy stores or any other stores for selling us ammo, bomb materials or anything like that because its not their fault, i dont want no fucking laws on buying fucking PVC pipes. we are kind of a select case here so dont think this will happen again. dont blame the school, dont fucking put cops all over the place just because we went on a killing spree doesnt mean everyone else will and hardly ever do people bring bombs or guns to school anyway, the admin. is doing a fine job as it is, i dont know who wll be left after we kill but damnit dont change any policies just because of us. it would be stupid and if there is any way in this fucked up universe we can come back as ghosts or what the fuck ever we will haunt the life out of anyone who blames anyone besides me and V. if by some wierd as shit luck my and V survive and escape we will move to some island somewhere or maybe mexico, new zelend or some exotic place where americans cant get us. if there isnt such place, then we will hijack a hell of a lot of bombs and crash a plane into NYC with us inside iring away as we go down. just something to cause more devistation.

Philosophy:

My belief is that if I say something, it goes. I am the law, if yo
u don't like it, you die. If I don't like you or I don't like what
 you want me to do, you die. If I do something incorrect, oh fucki
ng well, you die. Dead people cant do many things, like argue, whi
ne, bitch, complain, narc, rat out, criticize, or even fucking tal
k. So thats the only way to solve arguments with all you fuckheads
 out there, I just kill! God I cant wait till I can kill you peopl
e. Ill just go to some downtown area in some big ass city and blow
 up and shoot everything I can. Feel no remorse, no sense of shame
. Ich sage FICKT DU! I will rig up explosives all over a town and
detonate each one of them at will after I mow down a whole fucking
 area full of you snotty ass rich mother fucking high strung godli
ke attitude having worthless pieces of shit whores. i don't care i
f I live or die in the shootout, all I want to do is kill and inju
re as many of you pricks as I can, especially a few people. Like

America:

Love it or leave it mother fuckers. All you racist (and if you thi
nk im a hypocrite, come here so I can kill you) mother fucking ass
holes in America who burn our flags and disgrace my land, GET OUT!
 And to you assholes in iraq and iran and all those other little p
iece of shit desert lands who hate us, shut up and die! We will ki
ck your ass if you try to fuck with us or atleast I will! I may no
t like or government or the people running it or things like that,
 but the physical land and location I DO fucking love! So love it
or leave it!

Society:

I live in denver, and god damnit I would love to kill almost all o
f its residents. Fucking people with their rich snobby attitude th
inkin they are all high and mighty and can just come up and tell m
e what to do and then people I see in the streets lying their fuck
ing asses off about themselves. And then there is all you fitness
fuckheads saying shit like "yeah do 50 situps and 25 pushups each
morning and run a mile every day and go to the gym and work out an
d just push yourself to be better and you can achieve anything and
 set high goals and have great expectations and be happy and be ki
nd and treat everyone equal and give to charity and help the poor
and stop violence and drive safely and don't pollute and don't lit
ter and take shorter showers and don't waste water and eat right f
ood and don't smoke or drink and don't sell guns and don't be a ba
d person".......phew. I say "fuck you....shutup....and die...." And then pul
l the trigger of a DB#3 that is in your fucking mouth. All you fuc
king people with your set standard
s and shit, like you have to go to college and be smart and shit,
and you have to have a job and pay taxes, blah blah fucking blah,
shutup and DIE! I really don't give a good god damn about what you
 think is "right" and what is "wrong" and what is acceptable and w
hat isnt nice, I just don't fucking CARE! SHUTUP AND DIE!!!!!!!!

Ok people, I'm gonna let you in on the big secret of our clan. We ain't no god damn stupid ass quake clan! We are more of a gang. We plan out and execute missions. Anyone pisses us off, we do a little deed to their house. Eggs, teepee, superglue, busy boxes, large amounts of fireworks, you name it and we probably or already have done it. We have so many enemies in our school, therefore we make many missions. It's sort of a night time tradition for us.

Download CORRIDOR.MAP. It's a very close replica of the mission sites. But we have never seen the inside of the house… so we just guessed. It's also cut off where the area isn't important (Ya know, I didn't want to put in all of the neighborhood.)

The mission has been done. And the rebels… once again… emerged victorious. Vee falling blew de sheeeit outta loss stooff!!

As for the next mission, we haven't decided what to do or where to do it. I had some thoughts about hiding in some large bushes or trees and shooting stuff. Or maybe some more anal attacks. But we need to go up to Wyoming and load up on that stuff. We are running low. Plus, we just got our paychecks… they aren't big… but they can cover quite a bit of shit. We still need to get the fuses too. So far, the next mission will probably be in July sometime. But we AIN'T SURE.

MISSION LOGS:

6: Awwww yeya. This mission was so fuckin fun, man. Ok, first of all, my dad was the only parent home, so it was much easier getting out… but still hard since all these rocks in my backyard make so much noise. Plus the neighbors faulting dog barking its faulting head off. First we went through the corridor… going through some very tall grass fields… not as tall as the ones in the Lost World, but close. Felt kinda cool. Then we set up the strip of 1132 fire crackers. Using 2 cigarettes as starting fuses, we had plenty of time to spare. We also had a nice little crackering fountain hooked up to the fuses too. After a few minutes of setting it up, we lit it and went over and hid in on top of this big cement pipe going under a street. We were on the side of a hill so we hid in the grass. There was also a full moon that night, and not a foaming cloud in the sky. So it was like noon on the equator when we were out in the open. But, black clothing and tall grass sure helps. After about 5 minutes (forever) it began. Beforehand we watched as some lights in the Target's house went on… then off. Maybe the bastard heard something. But when the strip started, he turned his bedroom lights off. The strip lasted for about 30 seconds… we think… it was very fucking long. Almost all of it went off. Loud and bright. Everything worked exactly how we wanted it to. After about 15 minutes, we started down the bike trail to the next target. The first target's lights were on again in the bedroom,

but we think we got away undetected. While we were walking to the
next target, we shot some stuff. Heh, VoDkA brought his sawed off BB
gun and a few BB's too. So we loaded it, pumped it, and fired off a
few shots at some houses and trees and stuff. We probably didn't do
any damage to any houses, but we aren't sure. The gun was not loud at
all, which was very good. At the next target, we set up the saturn
missile battery and the rockets. These both has fuses about 2-3 feet
long. I lit them as VoDkA and KiBBz were over hiding in the shadows.
Luckily there were some trees and stuff at the 2nd target so we could
hide pretty good. Anyway, I lit and went over to the others. We
watched as the fuses burned and burned… then the rockets went off. It
was pretty nice, not so much meant as a prank, but more as a nice
little fireworks show. They made some noise, but nothing to shit yer
pants about. But the battery didn't work. So I went back, checked it
out, and the fuse had burned down to about 2 inches, so I just said
up yours baby and lit it. Right as I made it to the others it went
off. It was pretty quick, and loud too. Since the missiles are
whistlers, they probably woke up a few residents. YEY. Then we
started heading up to this construction site. It's right on the side
of a kinda busy road, but before the houses. We dodged a few cars,
messed around at the site. And we also swiped some signs from this
fence that was put up around the soon-to-be-foundation of whatever is
being built. The signs read "RENT-A-FENCE" and had some 1 800 number
on them. So we got some very nice souvoneers (spelled close enuf)
from that place. Then, as KIBBz and VoDkA were down in the foundation
hole and I was up on top, a cop drove by. We had enough time to see
it, take cover, and watch it go by, so it didn't get us by surprise.
But once we saw it was a cop we decided it was time to farming LEAVE.
He didn't stop, he drove right by, but @#%$ he mighta been looking
for us. So we got out of the fence, grabbed our signs and went to the
neighborhood again. We didn't have that much trouble getting back
home, just some dogs and @#%$. Once we got in, we were tired as a
priest after a 5 hour orgy. The total mission took about 3 hours. We
left around 12:30 and got back around 3-3:30. We aren't very sure,
but it lasted a while. And damnit, it was well worth it. We needed
that mission too, we were all pretty tired of waiting and our nerves
were just about shot. So it was perdy relaxing to be free like that.

5: This mission was one of the best we ever did. This was from
Kibbz's house to several locations in his neighborhood. That night
was probably the longest walk we ever did. First we went to this
soccer field/playground. It was right on the corner of a very busy
intersection. So every minute we had cars goin by. There was a lot of
moonlight that night, We got to the playground and dodged the lights
of cars for about 20 minutes. Then we decided what our first strike
would be like. We got a big McD's cup, and went to center field of
the soccer field. We got out about 20 bottle rockets that were
stripped together, and a 100 somethin strip of blackcats. Each had

very good and long fuses so we had lots of time. We lit them, and ran over and got in front of these big pine trees. We were totally out of vision. The rockets went off first. They launched out over the field and then the strip went off, after that we started goin back the way we came. Which went through this trail about 35yards wide with houses on either side. We found this large metal tub… perfect for firecrackers!!! We decided that Kibbz and Vodka would walk off toward the street on the other side of the trail and hide behind some trees while i lit it. Except… the street was over 100 yards away. And they were about 15 yards past it. Once they signaled me, I lit the small assortment of thunder bombs and about 50 stickless bottle rockets. They would only make sound, no visual effects. But anyway, I lit and sprinted the whole f*ckin way. About 3/4ths the way the fireworks went off, I was right in the middle of this big ass trail. I never ran so fast in all the missions. But I made it to the others and watched all these lights go on from the houses. Then we walked over to this big open hill between some houses and a busy street. We got a long wooden board and placed it on the hill. We had a long strip of about 200 and a little brick of about 3 packs of thunder bombs. This time we used a cigarette fuse. We only needed about an inch of it. We lit the cigarette and went over to hide behind some trees. When it went off, it was VERY loud where we were so we bolted outa there. After a few minutes we went back to see if all the stuff had gone off and it all did. So we got some souvaneers (i know misspelled) and went home. Drank some Aftershock that night too. We were supposed to have a few chicks come with us, but they couldn't make it… so maybe next time.

4: This mission was frehkin unique. The mission was from my house (REB), through the corridor, past the graves, and to the place where we do all of our fireworks. It was supposed to be like the other missions to this place. The weather was nice, we had 4 items made up and ready for use. The first fuse didn't work. The second fuse malfunctioned also. Both of those items were just about 100-120 thunderbombs stripped together. We had one more like the first 2 and we also had a little contraption of bottlerockets. These bottle rockets were stripped together, and put into a bottle. We placed this bottle on top of a large hill. So quite a few people could see. After about the 3rd try, I decided to just light the fuses that were directly from the rockets. Usually we use loooong fuses so we have time to get away. But this time, with Vodka and Kibbz standing over in front of some big ass shrubbery. I just did the direct fuse. After lighting it, I ran like a sonuvabitch to Vodka and Kibbz. By the time I made it to them the rockets were starting to go off. We had about 50 in the assortment, so it lasted a while. It was rather perrrty. Then we busted the bottle and went BACK to the 2 strips that didn't work.They both had rather crappy quality fuses so they went out before they reached their target. I took the last one, tied the remainder of the first 2 fuses to it, and lit it for the final f*ckin time. Since I am the fastest in the group, I usually light the fuses and Kibbz would be at the point where we stop running. Vodka would keep guard while I light. This time both of them went over and laid down on the side of this hill about 100 yards away. This would be the first time we have ever seen our own work in action. All the other times we just heard them. I lit it, ran to the hill, and watched the lovely ass fireworks go off. They lasted about 45 seconds, a total of around 400 went off. Dogs were barkin and everything. It was really cool to see em all too. After that we went to this point in the trails that looked like the Q from quake. We smoked some cigars, and headed home. Except… when we were a few blocks away from home, we had an incident. We were walking along the sidewalk when a f*cking garage door opened at the house that we were right by! We bolted into that persons yard… and ducked down and tried to be as quiet as possible. This adult came out, got his newspaper (it was about 4:30 in the AM) and went back in. I tried to signal Vodka and Kibbz, but they didn't see me. We waited… a few minutes later the man got in his car and started down his driveway. The flood of lights from his car just covered us. He stopped, got out, and yelled "WHO ARE YOU!" We got up, said we were just passin through and stuff, and he kept sayin "GET OUT OF HERE", "ILL CALL THE COPS!" and "WHO ARE YOU." We f*ckin hauled assholes and elbows home. This mission was also liquor free as a result of this person named Brooks Brown (phone #) who tried to narc on us. Telling my parents that I had booze and @#%$ in my room. I had to ditch every bottle I had and lie like a f*ckin salesman to my parents. All because Brooks Brown thought i put a little nik in his windshield from a snowball… BS? Yes. Anyway, that was mission 4.

3: This mission was an attack on the people who shot Vodka's bike, and on some random houses. First, after sneaking out of my house at around 1:55, we lit off 1 strand of 200 thunder bombs and 6 bottle rockets. We had also set a time delayed assortment too. This was made of 10 bottle rockets and a few crackering balls. We aren't really sure if those went off though because by the time they would have, we where a mile away. After the fireworks, we went over to this asshole's house. His name is brooks brown (phone #) (address). If any of you feel like pranking him. Anyway, we didn't really do much to him. Just put some model puddy on his Merc. Then, we went to another kid's house, and started to teepee his big, tall, thick, thorny-ass-tree. We set off the motion detectors about 4 times, and we dodged 1 car. But we didn't get caught! His tree was completely covered and wrapped in ass whiping paper. Even though we only had 4 rolls, we did one helluva good job. After that we moved some rather large rocks onto peoples driveways and tagged RC into a fence. Then, we came home and got drunk while watching Bordello of Blood.

2: Our second mission was against this complete and utter fag's house. Everyone in our school hates this immature little weakling. So we decided to "hit" his house. On Friday night (2/7/97) at about 12:15AM we arrived at this queer's house. Fully equipped with 3 eggs, 2 roles of toilet paper, the cheap brand, no pretty flowers. (we were disappointed to) superglue, and the proper tools to make his phone box a busy box (for those of you that are stupid, a buy box is where you set their box so that when they try to make a call, they get a busy signal and when someone else calls, they get a busy signal too). We placed 2 eggs in his very large, thick bushes. We just barely cracked them open so they will be producing a rather repulsive and extremely BAD odor for sometime. We placed the last egg on his "welcome" mat. It was very neat, I cracked the egg, put the yoke in the center, and the 2 halves on either side of the yoke. Then we teepeed his large pine tree and this… oak? tree. I don't know, it's big though. It wasn't a complete teepee but it was enough to agitate the home owner greatly. We also put the superglue on the front door and on the little red mail box flag.

1: The first was when we put an entire assortment of very loud fireworks in a tunnel, and lit them off at about 1:00AM. This mission was part of a rebellion against these assholes that shot one of our bikes one day. They were rather angry that night, and we were very happy. We will be doing another hit on their house sometime in the near future. And that one will be much closer. And louder.

After each mission we get drunk. Not with wimpy beer, we only use hard liquor. Aftershock, Irish Cream, Tequila, Vodka, Whiskey, Rum, and sometimes a few shots of EVERCLEAR. We also sometimes make up our own shooters. And sample others (never try a prairie fire, its killer!). In our next few missions, we are planning to hit the dorks house a few more times, along with a few other houses. And also set off some more fireworks at that tunnel. We each have a large supply of fireworks… loud ones… and soon I will have my license and we can drive around any place we want to. heh heh. Soon I will be putting our directions for mixing drinks that we make up. We will put up any good shooter or other drink that we try. So check this place out often.

R....e....b....e....l....C....l....a....n

this page was written by REB

REB VoDkA KIBBz

http://members.aol.com/rebdoomer/index.html

Wie gehts.

REBEL NEWS: Yo, this page will be getting some bigass changes soon. Ill be adding some new pages to it such as "New group names" and "Top 10 lists." Gonna have some cool shit. check it out. or ill blow you up. cause jo mamma............is so fat.

Homework sucks.

Mother fucker blew BIG. Pazzie was a complete success and it blew dee fuck outa a little creek bed. Flipping thing was heart-pounding gut-wrenching brain-twiching ground-moving insanely cool! His brothers havent found a target yet though.

Atlanta, Pholus, Peltro, and Pazzie are complete. for those of you that dont know who they are, they are, they are the first 4 true pipe bombs created entirely from scratch by the rebels (REB and VoDkA). Atlanta and Pholus are each 1 1/4" by 6" pipes, Peltro is 1" by 6", and Pazzie is 3/4" by 5". Each if packed with powder that we got from fountains, morter shells, and crackering balls. Each also has a +14" morter shell type fuse. Now our only problem is to find the place that will be "ground zero." Me and VoDkA also have made 2 more noisey crickets.

God damnit i'm sick of people saying "wick" when talking about fireworks! Don' falkin' say anothuh falkin' WICK or I's gone to rip yer falkin' HAID off and YOU-rinate down yo' falkin' neck!! ITS FUSE!

Special thanks to Excaluber, KiBBz, <Picture>, VoDkA, Jester, and Imaginos for helping me make this page happen.

Hey, the clan page is currently down. If you have a strong desire to learn about us, just mail me. Ill let yall know when i decide to put the page back up. (so dont even try to click on duh little thigy below!)

This will not work with AOL3.0's browser because aol sucks to much.

Remember, these pages are viewed best with Netscape or Microsoft Internet Explorer. Not with AOL's browser. It sucks.

http://members.aol.com/rebdomine/index.html

Wie gehts.

Well all you people out there can just kiss my ass and die. From n
ow on, i dont give a fuck
what almost any of you mutha fuckas have to say, unless i respect
you which is highly
unlikely. but for those of you who happen to know me and know that
 i respect you, may peace
be with you and dont be in my line of fire. for the rest of you, y
ou all better fucking hide
in your houses because im comin for EVERYONE soon, and i WILL be a
rmed to the fuckin teeth
and i WILL shoot to kill and i WILL fucking KILL EVERYTHING! No i
am not crazy, crazy is
just a word, to me it has no meaning, everyone is different, but m
ost of you fuckheads out
there in soceity, going to your everyday fucking jobs and doing yo
ur everyday routine shitty
things, i say fuck you and die. if you got a problem with my thoug
hts, come tell me and ill
kill you, because......god damnit, DEAD PEOPLE DONT ARGUE

God DAMNIT I AM PISSED!!

--_--
--_--_--

Remember, these pages are viewed best with Netscape or Microsoft I
nternet Explorer. Not with
AOL's browser. It sucks.

School Work

Eric Harris

perio4

9\22\95

THE HANGOUT

In the small, rural town of Phillipsburg on the border of a large, tall forest, a group of 6th grade boys are hanging out near a small shopping plaza. Dave, a five foot seven blond boy was talking with his two best friends, Danny and Bill.

"Hey Danny, uh, me and Bill were wonderin' if uh, if you wanna go out in the woods after school and look for a new hangout place?"

"Yeah, I guess. I mean these guys are fine, but I think we should find a hangout place just for us three," said Danny quietly.

"I know what ya mean, I'm getting sick of John and his little sidekick Joe. It's like they're joined at the hip almost." I whispered. I did not want John and Joe to hear this little conversation.

Danny was a short kid, about five feet. He has the most wicked eyes I have ever seen. Maybe like some sort of a demons' eyes or something. His short buzz-cut made him look like a mini-marine with glasses. Bill, on the other hand, was about my height and is pretty large. His hair-cut is as if he stuck his head out of a car window for a while and then added a lot of hair spray. And out of the two of them, Bill is the brave one, not to bright but brave.

"Oh, Danny, bring your firecrackers in case someone from the gang follows us. If we even find anything," said Bill, the pyro in the group.

The next day we left our houses and went out into the tall forest to look for a new hangout place. Some of the trees in there must be at least a hundred feet tall. The large, almost majestic trees swayed in the light spring breeze. As we traveled through this giant forest we came to a stop at the largest, fattest, most oddly shaped oak tree we have ever seen. Its' snake like arms twisted and pushed through all the other trees surrounding it. And they were surrounding the tree, almost as if protecting it from some monster. When we saw this tree and its branches running around everywhere Danny said, "I think we just found a new hangout place."

We had. We used the low branches to sit and do homework on and all the others to mess around on. The tallest branches are reserved for a kind of a lookout tower for any of the old gang guys coming to take what is ours. After about ninety minutes of messing around we went home.

The next day at school we were talking about whether or not we should put any traps around the oak, that's what we call the place, for any intruders.

"I think we should because John and his gang walk close to there every day and they might hear us one day and try to takeover our place." I said to Bill and Danny.

"Yeah but we might trip on them ourselves, ya know," said the always safe Danny boy. "And besides, they would probably see all of the traps."

"Then we cover them up good and make a map of where they are or something." Bill said.

"Make a map of where what are?" Asked John, who we didn't even see walk by.

"Nothing John, we were just talking about our homework," said Danny, as he fought to come up with another excuse.

"Liar. I heard about the new hangout that you guys found and starting tomorrow, we're gonna hangout there too, because that place sounds pretty cool," said John confidently.

"I don't think so John, that is our place, not yours and only we hang out there. And we will defend it if you try and go there." I remarked.

"Fine then, we'll fight you for it! And were gonna kick your butts." And then he left.

"Great man, just great, were gonna be buried at the oak if we don't let them go there!" Danny said as he panicked.

"I don't think so Danny boy" I said, thinking of a way to defend our, well our fortress now.

That day after school we set up trip wires, ditches, and a covered river all around the front of the oak. The thick, twisting branches of the oak tree and the smaller siblings around it formed an organic barricade and wall. We even brought in our new paint ball guns. With four buckets filled with up with paint balls and a small box of assorted fireworks, we were ready to kick some butt!

The next day at school we could only think about the fight that afternoon. I was thinking that we would win in the end. But I heard that they had some paint ball guns of their own and that all of Johns friends were coming. The feeling before the battle was one I never felt before. It was a mix between anticipation, hope, fear, and wonder. If we didn't win, we would be laughed at for the rest of sixth grade and John would have his buddies pick on us every second.

After school we went to the oak and began to prepare for battle. About fifteen minutes later we saw them coming. We slapped down our protective visors and put on our masks for the paint balls. We fired a warning rocket in the air above them. They responded with a barrage of red and yellow paint balls that splattered all around us. Bill and Danny were at the bottom of the tree and I was at the top. I shouted "you asked for it!!!" and began to fire off a couple of paint balls.

Bill screamed out "Let's rock!" and fired about fifty balls out of his fully automatic paint ball gun.

Danny and I both fired a twelve pack of bottle rockets out of our little guns made to fire the rockets. We made them out of a foot long pipe and a little wooden handle. A couple of them must have exploded close to them because we heard a couple "OW!"s and "AAAH!"s. As I fired more balls of paint I saw Joe trip over a trip wire and fall into our little man-made pond, which was obscured from his vision by leaves at the time. He was so embarrassed of his unexpected swim that he began to get up and run away. I fired about twenty balls that hit him as he scurried away.

After about ten minutes of steady barrages of paint balls and explosions from our pyrotechnics the only person that was left was John and a friend of his, Matt. Matt was only about ten meters from the closest branch of the oak tree when I grabbed three strips of two hundred firecrackers. I lit one after another and tossed them at him. After he ran away we had to deal with John. He had just got onto the first tree branch when Danny popped up and stared at him with those animal like eyes. John seemed hypnotized so me and Bill surrounded him and blasted his face with paint balls. Danny then launched a potato from our secret weapon, the potato gun and it hit him in the stomach and he fell off the branch, staggered up, and started to run. As he ran, we unloaded the rest of our paint balls on them, about sixty bottle rockets and about five potatoes from our potato gun.

We had won. The oak tree was ours for the keeping. The injuries were light, Bill was hit in the shoulder with a bottle rocket and Danny was shot in the left forearm with what appeared to be a pellet. Someone must have had a pellet gun. On the contrast, I was bruised in the shoulder when a broken branch fell on it. All of us were bruised and dripping with paint except Danny, who had only one hit in the foot.

When we went out into the battlefield we found six paint ball guns covered in green paint, which was the color of Danny's paint balls. Another gun had a bottle rocket stuck in the barrel, one of Danny's rockets.

"Gees Danny, you went berserk here. You must have hit these guns ten times each," I said in amazement.

"Yeah I guess I did lose it a little."

After that day we went to that enormous oak tree every afternoon. We never had to defend it again and John became the school dork. The hangout was ours.

NAME POEM
ERIC DAVID HARRIS

Enticing
Ready to help
Intriguing
Careful

Daffy
Amazing
Victorious
Intelligent
Dependable

Humorous
Artistic
Rebel
Reliable
Imaginative
Sarcastic

-ERIC HARRIS-

I AM POEM

Eric Harris
per. 6
10\30\95

I am a nice guy who hates when people open their pop can just a little.
I wonder what my soccer team will be like in the Spring.
I hear myself turning on the ignition of an F-15.
I see myself flying above everyone else.
I want to fly.
I am a nice guy who hates when people open their pop can just a little.

I pretend I am walking on the moon.
I feel that I will get straight A's again.
I touch the sky.
I worry that I will have a fire in my house.
I cry when I see or hear a dog die.
I am a nice guy who hates when people open their pop cans just a little.

I understand how to play soccer.
I say that a sport is something that you have to break a sweat in.
I dream that I am the only person on Earth.
I try to be as nice as I can.
I hope there isn't another O.J. trial.
I am a nice guy who hates when people open their pop cans just a little.

Some interesting ideas. variety!

58

NARRATIVE POEM

Eric Harris
per. 6 11\2

The big game has finally come tonight.
The Columbine Rebels versus the Chatfield Chargers in football.
The Chargers are filled with fright,
For the Rebels will beat them like a rag-doll.

Coach Lee of the Chargers was a nervous guy.
But when the kickoff came, and the Rebels began to boast,
Coach Lee almost died,
Because the football had landed beside his own goal post.

During the first quarter,
Rebel quarterback ███████████ threw three touchdown passes.
Plus the Rebel defense was like a mortar,
And the Charger offense pilled up in masses.

The second and third quarter were boring.
There was very little scoring.
But when the two-minute warning was reached,
The Rebel defense was breached.

The Chargers had scored a touchdown,
Which gave the Rebel defense a frown.
Although the score was twenty-one to seven,
Coach Lee felt that he was in heaven.

The game is exciting now,
Coach Lee and the Chargers scored two more touchdowns.
But it appears that ████████ is coming in.
And he is as mad as sin.

███████ throws a touchdown pass right away,
And now the Chargers don't want to play.
For ██████ is here to stay,
And the Chargers are dead in this fray.

████████ s now part of Rebel Fame.
The final score was forty-nine to seven in that game.
Coach Lee walked off the field that day staring at his feet and the pebbles,
Too depressed to look up because of his defeat by the Rebels.

Eric Harris
period 2
2\12\96

SIMILARITIES BETWEEN ZEUS AND I

The Greek god Zeus is most similar to me for many reasons. First, I try to settle problems in a mature, non-violent manner and so does Zeus. The second reason is that I often try to create new things. Therefore I am like Zeus because he is the ruler of the gods and creates new rules and animals. The next reason is that Zeus and I both like to be powerful and have some control over what is happening. I am always asking questions or double-checking myself to be sure I completely understand something so I am in control. We also both like to be leaders of large groups of people. I usually turn out to be a great leader just like Zeus. Zeus and I also get angry easily and punish people in unusual ways. For example, Prometheus stole the gift of fire and was then punished in an unusual manner. I usually punish people in unusual ways who steal or make me angry. The last reason I feel I am like the god Zeus is that we both are kind to other animals or people. All these reasons show why Zeus is the Greek god most similar to me.

Eric Harris
Sphere
Michael Crichton
371 pages

BOOK REPORT

Sphere, by Michael Crichton, is about a team of scientists in the Pacific Ocean. They were in an underwater naval habitat investigating a top secret discovery. The top secret discovery was an extremely large spaceship from an unknown origin. After discovering that the space ship was an American craft, they entered it and found a large sphere 30 feet in diameter. Later, one of the scientists entered the sphere and after he came out he was able to create his thoughts into actual objects. One problem was that the scientist did not know that he had this power.

In the novel, Sphere, I learned many different views on time travel, space, and time itself. I learned that gravity curves space and time. Also, I learned that a black hole in space can make tears in the fabric of time, allowing time travel. Another thing I learned is that under stressful and dangerous conditions many people may turn on one another in order to survive. I liked many things about this novel. One of such was the complete originality of the story line and plot. I also enjoyed how Michael Crichton kept the story going. All throughout the book the story stayed alive and never had any boring or dull parts. The main thing I would have improved about this novel was the origin of the spaceship and the sphere. I wish that Michael Crichton would have told me more about the background of the spaceship and how the sphere got on the ship.

Eric Harris
The Lost World
Michael Crichton
Number of pages, 393

BOOK REPORT

In The Lost World, the sequel to Jurassic Park, a team of scientists discovers an island inhabited by genetically engineered dinosaurs. However, when the scientists try to study the dinosaurs' habits and life styles, the dinosaurs attack. As a result, several people are killed.

In this book, I learned many different ideas for the theory of evolution, such as the theory that all life was created by an alien life form. I Also learned about a theory that all life is meant to become extinct sometime. Another theory I learned is that you can not study a habitat without having an effect on it. The best parts of The Lost World were when the author used his writing skills to tell me the description of a scene. Michael Crichton's use of adjectives and verbs completely put the scene into my mind and in implicit detail. The only thing I believe the author could have done to make the book better was to have a more conclusive ending. The ending leaves you hanging and wondering what happens to the dinosaurs. So, unless the author is preparing the reader for another sequel, the ending could have been improved.

Eric Harris

period 1

2/18/97

Mrs. Caruthers

In the course of my life, I have moved to different houses or locations about six times. The last three times I have moved, I left behind some of the greatest friends I ever had. Since my father was a United States Air Force pilot, we had to move often. It is always hard to leave close friends behind. And since most of them live on the other side of the country, I will probably never see many of them again. A few I stay in touch with, but most I have lost. It is hard loosing a friend, like Alexandra did in "O Pioneers." I will discus the last three places I have lived in and the friends and memories I have left behind. I have lived in two homes in Oscoda, Michigan and one in Plattsburgh, New York.

The first home I lived in was located in a largely wooded area, so we didn't have many neighbors. Oscoda is a very, very small town. Of the three close neighbors I had, two of them had children my age. Every day we would play in the woods, or at our houses. We would make forts in the woods or make them out of snow, we would ride around on our bikes, or just explore the woods. It was probably the most fun I ever had in my childhood.

After living there for 3 years, we moved to live on the Air Force base. It was hard leaving my friends, especially my best friend. Even though we were still only a 10 minute drive away, we only saw each other maybe three times after that. We lived on the Air Force base for about half a year. I made friends there, some were good, but none were as good as my friends at my old house. Since we lived on the base, we had lots of neighbors. The houses in those old bases are like a lot of small condos. My friends and I had a lot of fun there, too. We still lived close to a large wooded area so we would travel around in there almost every day. We were all the same age too, so that made it even more fun.

But, as our family knew, we moved that summer. This time we moved to Plattsburgh, New York. It was real hard leaving my friends again. And that time I had to say goodbye to my first best friend for good. Plattsburgh is in upstate New York, along the shore of Lake Champlain. Home of the Lock Ness Monster's cousin, Champy. We lived on an Air Force base there too. It wasn't as crammed as the one in Oscoda, but it was still small. At first I had no friends there, even though there was many kids my age.

Then once school started, and even some help from my older brother, I had some friends. It took a while for our friendships to grow, but soon we were best friends and did everything together. Kris████the best friend I ever had, lived about 2 blocks away. Every day we would find something new to do. Some days we would walk along the shore of the lake and just mess around there. Sometimes we would look for old bullet shells from around 50 years ago and we even looked for Revolutionary War and Civil War era items. Kris once found the diary of a slave under some old Civil War barracks. We also found buttons, bullets, old bottles of whiskey or other liquor, and even some items from some very old train wreck. We had quite the collection of items, which most of them I still hold today. Sometimes Kris and I would play baseball (actually it was just home-run derby) with our friend from Norway, Jens. Jens was a good friend, he was the shiest person I had ever known and he wasn't used to our American customs, but he was always there. Kris and I made it our mission to make Jens into a normal American kid. We would go to the base gym almost every day and just mess around there. The gym was a very large facility, complete with full basketball court, racquetball courts, and a running track *above* the basketball court. We spent countless hours there, just hanging out and talking. Kris and I would ride our bikes all over the base too, we loved to ride bikes and the base was just full of interesting places. Soon news came that the base was going to be closed. This prompted a major campaign. There were large public parties held and everything. Then came Independence Day. The base had a large field in the center of all the housing areas, and every year they would hold a spectacular fireworks show. Kris, Jesse, and I (our other best friend) had the best seats in the house. We were about 100 feet away from the launch site of these fireworks. So they were exploding right over our heads. Then later that night there was a large party with bands playing and singing. A few weeks later, Kris moved to Georgia. This was hard to swallow. We had spent more time together than we did with our own families, and now he was gone. I still had Jesse though. And with what little time I had left in Plattsburgh, we did as much as we could together. Then, after my dad retired from the Air Force as a Major, we moved to Denver, Colorado. It was towards the end of the summer, so Jesse and I had spent some good times together. It was the hardest moving from Plattsburgh. I have the most memories from there. When I left Jesse, and when Kris left, I had a lot of feelings. I felt alone, lost, and even agitated that I had spent so much time with them and now I have to go because of something I can't stop. It doesn't take long to make a best friend, but it only takes 2 words to loose one. Those are, "We're moving." I still stay in touch with Kris, and I try to with Jesse and some other friends from Plattsburgh. But there was a few that I didn't get phone numbers or addresses from. Such as my best friend in Oscoda.

Loosing a friend is almost the worst thing to happen to a person, especially in the childhood years. I have lived in many places, but the last three places have been the most fun and the greatest experiences of my childhood. Although memories stay with you, the actual friend doesn't. I have lost many great friends, and each and every time I lost one, I went through the worst days of my life. Since loosing a friend is something I have experienced many times, I know what Alexandra feels like in "O Pioneers." And it isn't something I would not like to feel for a long time.

Guns! Boy, I loved playing "guns" as a kid. It is one of the few things I miss from childhood today. Living in a rural town in Michigan for three years, I played a lot in a forest. My brother, two friends and I would always be running around shooting imaginary bad-guys. The woods behind my house were vast, empty, and old. It smelled of a musty tree or maybe of pine trees most of the time in there. Those woods left so many memories in the mind it's amazing. Such as how scary they looked during hard rain storms or how dark they were at night. I was even afraid to go into the woods during nighttime, for fear of the unknown. For the most part, however, my memories are fond ones. My brother, Sonia, and I had countless missions in those woods, hunting for enemy troops and stopping invasions. We would set up little tree fort made of loose sticks and branches, and use them for our bases and camps. "Fire!" I would scream, as we all made as many fast gun sounds as we could, waving our deadly plastic toys around. Almost every time we had a firefight, we would pretend one of us would be injured. We always would carry little bandages and tape with us to dress the wound. Luckily, the bullet would always go right through so we wouldn't need to perform surgery. Sonia, being her crazy self, would run right into the battle screaming and firing at all the bad guys, as we gave cover fire. It seemed to vivid, our fighting, and so real. Now that I have actually fired weapons I realize how unrealistic we were, but hey, we were just kids!

"Where's the air support?!" my brother screams, as I reload my M16. "Hell if I know!!" I retort. "We got more incoming APCs on our 6's, set those mines quick!" Sonia hollers. The bad guys were surrounding us, but we had plenty of ammo to last us for hours. I toss a few stick grenades into the trees ahead, and duck as they go off killing the wave of enemy troops. Kevin was setting the mines for those trucks and Sonia was launching rockets at the platoon on our left. "Grenade!" I scream as I see a stick fall in

our base. Sonia and I jump out over the tree trunks as the grenade destroys our base.

"We gotta move, now!" Sonia yells in my ear under all the shooting. We run right past

my brother and he joins up in the evacuation. Just then our air support flies by overhead.

"There's the gun-ships!" says my bro., as we dodge tree limbs, bullets, and mortars. We

stop at a group of rather large trees and turn and return fire. The air support is dropping

napalm on the advancing troops, and launching rockets at the trucks. We pull out a huge

machine gun and set it up on a stationary position in a tree. Sonia and Kevin start

spraying bullets everywhere as I use hand-to-hand combat on a few bad guys that made it

to us. By the time I finish them off with a really strong stick, it's time to go inside and do

some homework, and Sonia needs to go out to dinner with her family tonight, too. All in

a day's work as a kid, I guess.

      One of these days, real soon, I will call up Sonia and see if she still remembers

me. And see if those woods, our forts, and our hide-outs are all still there where I left

them over seven years ago.

Renaissance Essence

In the play <u>Cyrano de Bergerac</u>, written by Edmond Rostand, Cyrano displays a true renaissance essence. He displays a knowledge of poetry, words, feelings, a superb fighting and fencing talent, and extreme generosity. I myself display a variety of mental and physical skills that could classify me as a "renaissance" man. I am efficient in several sports, in writing, in speaking, and in thinking.

In sports, I have been known to play soccer, baseball, football, and even mountain biking. In the sport of soccer, I have played as an offensive and defensive player. These two positions are very different from each other, since offensive is attacking and defensive is defending. I have proven myself to be a superb player in both positions. As for baseball, I was an excellent out-fielder and excellent second baseman. These positions are very different from each other and I show a bit of the renaissance essence in the fact that I was good at both of the positions. Playing football and mountain biking are two very different sports from each other and from soccer and baseball. Being able to play them both with a bit of talent shows that I have some renaissance spirit in me.

In the field of writing I have been known to display several different writing techniques. Such as harsh, kind, gibberish, serious, dramatic, and several other kinds. I have written harsh and kind letters to friends. In later response they have said the letters were effective. I have been know to write and even speak plenty of gibberish and meaningless sayings. Serious and often dramatic essays and speeches have came from me, some speeches have even been inspiring. My writing and speaking techniques have varied day by day and essay by essay, so one could say that I have a bit of the renaissance spirit in me.

My thoughts are the most original and distinctive part of my character. The variety and degree of my thoughts makes me a definite renaissance man. Thinking of topics from love to hate, from anger to enthusiasm, and sorrow to joy. Thoughts are such a unique aspect of one's character that one can not really describe them in a short essay. However, I believe that everyone has a little bit of the renaissance spirit in them just from their thoughts alone.

Sacrifice

In the play <u>Cyrano de Bergerac</u>, Cyrano made many honorable and brave sacrifices. Such as when he gave up all of his money so the poepl in the theater would be happy or when he spent every day crossing enemy lines just to send a letter to Roxane, his secret lover. I myself can recall one such brave and valiant sacrifice I made in my lifetime. It was when I rode my bike across a one mile trail and back to get my friend out of trouble.

My friend Kris and I were riding our bikes across a dirt trail in a wooded area in upstate New York. We were about a mile into the woods when we found a large drainage pipe. We decided to go explore inside and about 5 minutes into it we ran into a wave of water that knocked us out of the pipe. I landed in a pond below and got a large cut on my right t high but Kris was caught in some fishing wire right outside the tunnel. After about ten minutes of tugging and pulling we decided that I should go and get a knife to cut the wire since Kris was so entangled in it. So I got onto my bike and peddled through the forest with one leg since my other leg was in too much pain from the cut. I made it to a boat house and found a fishing knife and returned to Kris. He was beginning to get worried about his situation because the water kept getting colder. Even though he was only in about a foot of it. I cut him loose and we both went back to his house and tended to our wounds. The cut on my leg was bigger than I first thought it was, I ended up needing 13 stitches and was left with a very impressive scar. Throughout my whole bike ride to get the knife and return I was in constant pain and agony. My entire leg was covered with blood and dirt and washing it off in the pond's water only hurt more because the pond did not exactly have pure clean uncontaminated water. This was my sacrifice. To save my friend in spite of my pain. I very well could have stayed and spent another half an hour untangling my friend, but his arm was starting to turn blue since his arm's blood circulation was cut off and I

did not think we had time to waste. Plus our parents wanted us back home soon, so we needed to

hurry for that reason too. Kris thanked me and was shocked that I did all that for him in spite of

my painful wound. That is my most noble sacrifice that I can remember.

Poems and Song Lyrics

"SON OF A GUN"

© 1996 KMFDM ENT. US PUBL.

This song, by the German techno-music group "KMFDM," is one of my most favorite

songs. This song shows the way I feel about myself sometimes and it also gives me energy and

adrenaline so I play this song before my soccer games and such. I have heard this song at many memorable points in my teenage life, so it therefor comes to mind on many occasions. That is

why this song means a lot to me.

"WASTE"

This song is not as important to me as the previous, but I still like it for its meaning. Some of it's lyrics are true to me, but some are not. I believe that these lyrics have a significant amount of meaning to them, so that is why I choose to include this song. It is one of my favorite songs, and I can remember many times when I have actually listened to this song instead of just "hearing" it and thought, "This does have some meaning to it." As opposed to just "hearing" a song, "listening" is when one understands and thinks about the lyrics, or at least, that is my point of view.

"STRAY BULLET"

© 1996 KMFDM ENT. US PUBL.

I believe that this song describes my actions and thoughts the best. I have often been described by my friends and even family as a "stray bullet." Jokingly, some people have said that I am a "juggernaut, dearest friend, worst enemy, anarchist" and several other sayings from this song. That is why I chose to include this song, because it has several things in common with me and my personality.

Quotes From the Play

"Why, yesterday I did not have so many friends!"

"I have told her, and she loves you."

"It seems too logical, I have missed everything, even my death!"

"The blood was his."

"And you gentlemen, remember now, no rescue, let me fight alone."

--Each quote is from <u>Cyrano</u>, each font symbolizes the feelings--

Understanding the Play: *Cyrano's tragic flaw*

In Edmond Rostand's play <u>Cyrano de Bergerac</u>, Cyrano has many talents and marvels. He is a poet, a fighter, a lover, a hater, a man of honor, and a man of secrecy. However, he does have one tragic flaw. In the play Cyrano has a rather enormous nose, and he is well aware of this. He looses his temper at anyone who attempts to laugh or make fun of his nose. He thinks that no one could ever love him for his looks and often insults himself about his own looks. He knows he is a great poet and can make women love him for his words, but when it comes to his physical appearance he hides in the shadows and behind others. When it came to his true love Roxane, he uses Christian and his good looks to write what he has always wanted to write to Roxane, and confess his love. But, through Christian he did all of this. So throughout almost the entire play Roxane believes that Christian is the man of her dreams since she receives such beautifully written letters and poems thought to be from Christian. In reality they are from Cyrano. Cyrano is afraid to admit his love to Roxane because he fears that his nose will lead to his downfall with her. Ironically, it did. But rather than Roxane loving only a man who has good looks and a superb writing mind, she falls in love with the soul of a man with such great writing and speaking skills that she had loved so much. Which was Cyrano. Cyrano was only able to confess his love to Roxane when he is about to die. Cyrano's beliefs of his nose and physical appearance being repulsive led to his downfall by only letting him confess his love to Roxane minutes before his death.

What grade I deserve: B+

I feel that I deserve a B plus on the assignment for a few reasons. One of which is the amount of time and effort I spent on my cover sheet and picture. I feel that one could not have more of a renaissance theme than that picture. I have filled all of the requirements except my last paper is about half of a page short. Grammatical and mechanical errors are things that I feel I could have corrected even more if I had spent more time on that part of the assignment. However, most of my time was spent in the cover picture and the first two papers along with the appearance of the total project. That is why I feel I deserve a B plus or a solid B on this paper.

Eric Harris

#1

The first quote I chose to write on is, "No one knows he is fortunate until he becomes unfortunate." In the book, this quote has a lot of significance. Such as when Reuven was in the hospital recovering from his wound. When he was looking outside at the people walking in the fresh air, he remembered how he took his everyday walks for granted. He took many things for granted in the beginning of the book. But when he was in the hospital, he realized how fortunate he was. One other thing he took for granted was his eyesight. His eyesight wasn't even something he ever paid much attention to, but once it was taken away, he realized how important it was and how much everyone takes it for granted. When he was in the hospital, he realized that he had lost many normal activities. Such as walking, seeing, reading, and to just be free. I believe that we all take things for granted. Then once we loose that privilege, we realize how fortunate we were. Personally, this quote is very true. I have had many experiences where something was taken away from me that I used every day. Such as when I had surgery on my chest. When I got back from the hospital, I couldn't do anything that involved using my chest muscles. This meant I barely could even laugh. I learned then how many things I took for granted.

#2

The second quote I chose to discuss is "Things are always what they seem to be, Reuven? Since when?" This quote is very significant in the novel because of Reuven and his prejudice against Danny and the Orthodox Jews. He thought, at first, that Danny was an evil, "snooty" person that wanted to kill him. Then later he realized that Danny was a very intelligent, thoughtful, and caring human being just like himself. There were many points in the novel in which things were not as they seemed. Such as when Danny hit the baseball at Reuvens' head. Reuven thought that Danny did it on purpose but he really wasn't aiming for Reuven. Another point in the novel might have been when was wearing his glasses at the baseball game in the beginning of the novel. He saw several things that to him, seemed bad or different, but later he sees that those things where normal just like him. Like Dov, the boy who ran into Reuven during the game. It seemed to Reuven that he was a mean bully, but later he sees him in the synagogue and sees that he is just like everyone else. Personally, this quote means a lot to me. I have had countless experiences in which I thought I was sure about something, then later it becomes the opposite of what I thought. Such as when I had a friend that at first, he seemed to be a normal friend just like my others. Then he lied and turned on me, for no reason, and tried to get me in trouble and trying to get money out of me. This is probably the best example in my life of this quote. I have learned in my life to never believe first impressions, and always look a little deeper, because things aren't always the way they seem.

Medea Quote

The quote I have chosen from the play "Medea" is when Medea says, "no, like some yellow-eyed beast that has killed its hunters let me lie down on the hounds' bodies and the broken spears." This quote shows that Medea wants to die fighting, be brave and courageous and not let her hunters take her without a struggle. This pertains to today's society because generally people who are in trouble or on the run think or want to think that they will not go out without a fight, and some people believe that they will be taken quietly and calmly, and not struggle at all. In the play, it is what the Greek women want Medea to do, be taken without a struggle, but she refuses.

Some people in today's society believe or want to believe that they are tough and strong. They that they will not go out without a fight and can be brave in the face of danger and apprehension. Then again, there are people who say and do go out with a fight and aren't captured easily, proving they are who they say. There are also people who do not fight or struggle when captured. Euripides wants the readers to believe that Medea is as strong as she says and that she will put up a fight in the face of danger, which in my views she would. There are several different types of people in today's world as there was in ancient Greece. Medea is the type of person that is tough and hard as "stone" as she is often referred to as. The Greek women are the types of people who are more calm and have less of a will to be free or stand up. It seems like today many people are like that too, and that the people who are like Medea are rare or hard to find. Which is what the case is in the play. Medea is a foreigner to Greece and is different from all the people there.

So in conclusion, Euripides' play "Medea" has several themes and ideas that still pertain to today's society. One example is the quote by Medea, "no, like some yellow-eyed beast that has killed its hunters let me lie down on the hounds' bodies and the broken spears." Medea is portrayed as the type of person that would not be captured without a fight and would make a stand. The Greek women in the play tell her not to stand up, therefor they are the kind of people that would not fight or be courageous. This is like today's society because it seems like there are a few people like Medea and the majority of the people are like the Greek women.

Wasting Money

by

Eric Harris

period 1

5/12/97

Mrs. Caruthers

In the story, The Great Gatsby, there were many different themes. One of the most outstanding themes was the use of money in society. The West egg was the middle class section of the community and the East is where the higher class lives. Nick, Tom, Daisy, and Gatsby all live in the higher class section. Many of them have used their money unconsciously or wastefully.

Gatsby used his money in many wasteful ways. Some of these ways might have seemed unimportant or insignificant, but when one looks back on the story, these acts will look strange. Such as, when Gatsby and friends rented a luxurious hotel sweet for a few hours. Gatsby also went flying in his expensive air plane often and acted as if it was no big deal. Since he never truly worked for his money, he doesn't know how to enjoy his money and spend it wisely.

Tom and Daisy also used their money wastefully. Most of all though, they were inconsiderate. Throughout the story Tom and Daisy treated their child as if she was a piece of furniture. They would call her down and look at her, then send her back up to her room. Never thinking about her feelings and her needs for love and care. The most likely cause for their actions is probably their money. Since they did not earn it by working, they were spoiled and their inconsiderate actions were just a side effect.

In F. Scott Fitzgerald's novel, The Great Gatsby, there was a wide use of themes. One of the larger themes was money. Many of the citizens living on the East egg used money quite wastefully. Since most of the rich people got their money by inheriting it, they do not know how to work or do any thing else by themselves. In my opinion, those people are inconsiderate, selfish and they do not deserve to be at the top of society.

Singapore.

By: Eric Harris

period 4

Mr. Webb

10/6/97

"No gum, nope. We can't chew any gum in Singapore," said Nixon as we talked about his hometown of Singapore. Nixon is 28 years old and is visiting the United States for training in his job at Gates Rubber Co. He wanted me to use his first name in this report instead of using his entire name, plus he said it was to hard to pronounce in English anyway! As he was explaining his hometown to me, I realized that Singapore is a lot like the United States. Business, sports, and recreation are all very similar. Although, religion and customs vary quite extensively. Geographically Singapore is very small, approximately 616 square kilometers. Its inhabitants refer to it as a "island-city" since the city itself covers most of the island.

Singapore has a tropical climate so the sports are mostly similar to American sports. Nixon has played soccer and softball in his hometown. Rugby, bad mitten, and basketball are also offered. "Soccer is most popular, softball is popular too, though," Nixon explains as he remembers his younger years. His city is fairly up to date as far as electronics and businesses are concerned. Their computers are basically the same speed as ours, and the car systems are fairly recent. Nixon himself does own a computer. Even though the business he works for provides an e-mail address, so he can be in touch with the rest of the world at almost any place. When asked what he did for fun in Singapore Nixon replied, "We shop, or go to bars." The night life in Singapore is very much like America. There are bars, theaters, movies, and malls to go to after work or school is over. Compared to Colorado, Singapore does not have skiing, snowboarding, or hockey. On the other hand, one can go on walks or go rock climbing on the island. Nixon does not own a car or even a bike, instead he uses the vast subway system in Singapore. The price of a car in Singapore is about three times the cost in America, plus there are many taxes and expenses that add to the overall cost.

Singapore has many customs and traditions that might seem unusual to Americans. Even though Nixon is the first son in his family, he is still pursuing his job. Usually in his city the first born stays with the parents after school is over. Nixon once replied, "maybe my sister would do that for me," when asked if he would have to go back soon and stay with his mother and father. The main religion in Singapore is Buddhism. Muslim, Christianity, and several others also play a role in his culture. Nixon is Buddhist, and believes in the ways of Buddha. Nixon briefly explained the beliefs and thoughts of his religion. One of the main points he made on Buddhism was, "the ones who follow the religion closely do not believe in having material possessions. Instead they spend their time meditating and thinking of peace and tranquillity." His hometown celebrates many holidays for many religions. Such as Christmas or Singapore's independence day. The government in Singapore is a republic. The laws are somewhat similar to America. Although, some of the punishments are different. Some of the laws that are very different from America are that one can not chew gum, consume tobacco products, or drive under 16 years of age. The legal limit for alcohol is 18 years old. To buy an apartment in the city, one must be married or scheduled to be married within two years. Then, after the apartment is signed over, the couple must stay married for five years in order to keep their home. This is why most young adults live with their parents. As of right now, Singapore does not have a limit on the amount of children one couple can have. In the past, the law has been as low as one child per couple because the city was getting too crowded. When Nixon was asked if he was married he replied, "not yet, no. No interest in marriage yet." There are many limits on seeing movies. Movies with violence or sex in them are usually restricted to persons under 21. Pornography is completely outlawed in Singapore, along with fireworks. The Internet services on Singapore are monitored so people do not receive illegal files or information. The food in Singapore is mainly very healthy. There are traditional Chinese and Asian dishes along with the ever-popular Mc Donalds restaurants. The average work day is the same as the American work day. Usually a person will stay with the same company for their entire career. If one is fired or quits, they are hated or shunned. So when Nixon was asked if he would stay with the Gates Rubber Company he said, "I sure hope so!" One thing Nixon noticed about American people is that they are much more open minded and they speak their mind more than he is used to. Most of the citizens in Singapore are quite and keep to themselves. Americans, on the other hand, are free to do and say what they want, and according to Nixon, we do it all the time! He is surprised how much the people in America like to be individualists. "Some of the people here might even be arrested in Singapore for some of the things they do in public," said Nixon as we talked of the restrictions in his city.

The island of Singapore is located on the equator and around the tip of Malaysia. Which is south of Thailand. The climate is tropical, so there are hot summers and mild winters. Nixon knew a great deal of information on his hometown, so that led me to believe that he was proud to be from there. Singapore is not very much of an agricultural economy, rather more of business and electronics. Since the island is near two major bodies of water, it is known to have many busy harbors. When asked if he has ever been on a boat though, Nixon said, "No, I do not like boats too much." He gets around this little problem by flying to wherever he needs to go. The island does have an airport, and it is used quite often because of all the business traveling. Nixon said he would be returning to his home in early October. "I do like America, but I still think Singapore is better," said Nixon proudly.

In conclusion, Singapore is a very interesting place. From my new friend Nixon, I learned that his culture is very similar to Americas. We have many of the same sports, businesses, and entertainment methods. The religions and customs vary greatly between our two nations, but the moral values and legal standards are basically the same. Nixon is a good friend, and a very intelligent man. I enjoyed talking with him and I hope he will return to "our little country" soon. In the few hours I spent with him and his roommates, I learned that people from all over the world are all interested in the American ways of living and thinking, but it seems that we ourselves sometimes are not as interested in them. I believe that we should spend more time learning about other nations instead of being contempt with our own.

Guns in

Schools

Thorough & logical. A few formatting problems, however. Nice job. 69/75

By:

Eric Harris

period 4

12/10/97

Mr. Webb

Eric Harris
12/10/97

Guns in School

In the past few weeks there has been news of several shootings in high schools. A student in Texas killed three fellow classmates and injured many more when he fired at a prayer group before school. This student had several other weapons with him when he was apprehended, showing how easy it was to bring so many weapons to school and not be noticed. Students who bring guns to school are hardly ever detected. This is shocking to most parents and even other students since it is just as easy to bring a loaded handgun to school as it is to bring a calculator. *ouch!* The problem of guns in school is a major one faced by many parents, teachers, and citizens these days. Solutions are hard to come by in such a situation because of how widespread the problem is and how different each school in each town can be. Students can get weapons into school too easily and they have to much access to weapons outside of school.

A. Weapons in school are hard to detect and students have ways of getting out of searches or other ways of detection.

    1. One example of students avoiding detection is a 1990 survey conducted by the Centers For Disease Control (CDC) which found that one in 20 high school students carried a gun in school during the past month (CDC).

    2. Students can use their backpacks, purses, or even projects to bring weapons into school.

    3. Metal detectors can be avoided by using other school entrances.

B. Students have access to many weapons and can obtain a gun from many places.

    1. The low price of junk guns (as low as 69 dollars) brings these guns within the economic reach of children (Gun Digest, 288).

92

2. "Junk Guns," also known as Saturday Night Specials, are handguns that are extremely small, inexpensive and typically poorly made (Junk Guns).

   a. The fact that these guns are small and inexpensive implies that these "junk guns" can be found and purchased easily by students.

3. School security experts and law enforcement officials estimate that 80% of the firearms that students bring to school come from home, which shows where most students get their weapons. (Harrington 22).

Guns in schools are a growing problem in today's society. Every day the news broadcasts stories of students shooting students, or going on killing sprees, or even just bringing a gun to school. Students bring guns to school for many reasons. Some for protection, some for attacking, and even some to show off. However, a school is no place for a gun. Solutions for this problem are hard to come by and often too expensive for most schools to even consider, however metal detectors and more police officers are two very good solutions.

Metal detectors posted at entrances in schools can prevent guns from entering schools. That is a given fact. Although, the cost of these machines are rather high and some schools simply can not afford them. Tax payers and donations are other ways to form money to buy detectors, but some tax payers would not be happy with the prices. Several schools in the United States have metal detectors, and shootings still take place in the school. Students can be very resourceful, and can find ways to avoid the detectors. The idea of more police officers is a very good solution. However, this would also cost more money for the tax payers. The end result, in my opinion, is worth every penny spent.

Metal detectors and other forms of detectors are very good solutions. Once installed in all main entrances, students can simply walk through while trained officers can search suspicious bags and backpacks if the alarm goes off. Students will be much more safe, but the fact of low morale is still present. One problem with metal detectors is that several school-related items are metal and would most likely set off the alarm. This leads to several searches that turn up nothing. This can cause long lines and be a hassle for students trying to get to class.

Police officers can discourage students from bringing weapons and can stop anyone who manages to get a weapon in the school. They are there to protect and serve, so students can go to them if they want to report someone with a gun or any other incident. More cops in schools is a great start to preventing more shootings in schools. On the other hand, the more cops in a school the more it begins to look like a prison. The community does not want it's schools looking like jail houses with the children as the prisoners. They are there to learn and, if students feel uncomfortable, that only leads to more problems. Drop-outs, grades, and student morale would all get worse with the presence of police, even though the cops are there for the students safety. Therefor, only a few cops should be assigned to schools at first. The schools should let the officers and the students get familiar with each other. This familiarity will help the morale of the student body.

More and more we hear of shooting sprees and rampages on the news. Some can be prevented, some can not. Almost any school shooting could have been prevented in some way or another, we just have to spend the necessary time and money to figure out how. Metal detectors and more police officers are only two good solutions. If tax payers can afford to do one or both of these solutions, then that is fantastic. If not, then the community needs to figure out other ways to keep guns out of schools. Students can not learn very well and be motivated if they know that someone in their classroom has a gun with them. In conclusion, metal detectors and more police officers are a great start to the fight against guns in school.

Works cited

Centers For Disease Control. "Weapon Carrying Among High School Students." Morbidity and

Morality Weekly Report. Vol. 40 No. 40. 11 Oct. 1991.

Gun Digest 1995, 49th Annual Edition. Northbrook, Il. DBI Books, Inc., 1994. 288.

Harrington, Donna. "Blown Away." The American School Board Journal. May, 1992. 22.

"Junk Guns." On-line. Available: www.gunfree.org/csgv/bsc_jun.htm. 9 Dec. 1997

Return From the Stars

by: Stanislaw Lem

Novel Project

Eric Harris

period 5

Mr. Webb

4/27/98

The science fiction novel, <u>Return From the Stars</u> by Stanislaw Lem, is a story of an

astronaut named Hal Bregg who returns from a voyage that was ten years long for him and his

crew and 150 years long for Earth. Society has drastically changed and he is haunted by

memories of his dead crew members.

The story begins in an absolutely stunning description of a futuristic city as Hal Bregg

wanders around in it. For hours he explores the new and amazing city, lost and confused by all

the new customs, procedures, and strange people. He soon is confronted by a woman and Bregg

tries to explain to her about his background. The woman is frightened by his size which is larger

and more muscular than everyone else in the city and shocked that he is not "betrizated," which

is a process all humans and other evolved life forms go through at birth to nullify any violent

impulses or harmful actions. Bregg then goes to a hotel and searches for any old friends or

people that he might know or that might be able to explain what has happened to Earth.

After talking to a few doctors and scientists he discovers that all his work was for

nothing. Almost half of his crew died for barely anything useful. Space exploration was deemed

unimportant and wasteful. All sports and physical competitions ceased to exist because the were

too dangerous. Any records set would only be broken by men or women that were not normal or

were genetically enhanced, all human limits were reached and humans stopped striving for

anything better. Remaining sports were padded to the point of which they were almost comical

for Bregg to view. The human race lost all sense of romanticism and adventure.

Bregg is crushed by this news. He attempts to surround himself with whatever he can

that remained from his time. He purchases books, (which were almost impossible to find since

no books had been published for fifty years), and finds an antic car, which still was futuristic to

that all cars, planes, trains, and any other forms of transportation have been deleted or changed so

that absolutely no risk is involved for humans. Cars are replaced by "gleeders," which are

described as flying black cigars. Several other ways of transportation are changed to be more

efficient and safer.

Anything that posses a threat to humans is done by robots. Hal Bregg learns that robots

are a major part of society. He learns that robots create, supervise, repair, and destroy

themselves and no human intervention is required any more. He learns from a famous author

and scientist that space travel is pointless since it takes so long to reach another solar system and

get back that by the time the ship has returned, Earth has changed so dramatically that none of

the information gathered is worth anything. Also, the author states that the odds of finding

another advanced civilization are very small, and that even if one was found, by the time the ship

returns to earth, the earth has changed drastically and then all the information that was gathered

by the crew of the ship is useless because the alien civilization has changed too. Bregg is

angered by his readings.

With the arrival of one of his crew mates, Olaf, he begins to feel better and not so alone.

Olaf and Bregg talk of their time on the voyage and recall all that they have been through and

what has happened to each other after they got back to Earth. Bregg is continuously haunted by

memories and flashbacks of his dead crew mates, and tells the reader about how each one died

and how he was involved in the death. After a love affair with a married woman who has mixed

feelings for Hal but still cares for him, Hal tries to commit suicide in his car but is stopped by

Eri, his lover. Hal leaves Eri and goes to see one of his other surviving crew mates, Thurber.

After talking with Thurber for a while Hal learns of another space expedition that has been

planned out in complete secrecy from the public. While deciding to leave Earth again or to stay with his new wife Eri, Hal runs away into the mountains. There, he climbs to the top of a small mountain and looks over on the city and ponders about life, the human race, and the expedition, and finally decides to return to Eri.

Return From the Stars is an extremely well written novel even though it has been translated twice, Russian to German and German to English. The novel has some of the best descriptive scenes I have ever read, it possesses several very absorbing ways of thinking and philosophical views on life and humanity, and it has several greatly thought-out views on space travel and science.

In the beginning of the novel Stanislaw Lem describes an amazingly advanced city with all new forms of buildings, transportation, lighting, architecture, and several other things. The characters perception of this new world along with the vast and expressive description of this world adds up to place a brilliant picture into the reader's mind. I read the first twenty pages with out even flinching I was so engrossed. Lem creates a whole new world and transports the reader to this place. His use of descriptive words and analogies are fantastic, along with his ability to let the character wander in his own thoughts and react to the environment. The scenes in which Hal Bregg has flashbacks of his mission and when some of his crew members were killed are beautifully written also. His description of space, planets, and the ship are spectacular. His descriptions are so life-like and well written that sometimes I forget that I am reading a book and it is not real.

This book made me think. That is putting it lightly. Since the descriptions are so detailed and brilliant and it seems so real it made me think about what it would be like to be there and what the other characters are thinking and several other things. During the story, the main character, Hal Bregg, reads several articles and books on what he missed while he was away.

Some of the things that he reads are most interesting. He reads about a process called "betrization." This process was started about twenty years after Hal left Earth. What it does is it neutralizes strong impulses and nullifies immoral thoughts. It becomes simply impossible for one to imagine harming another. This process is also used on animals, too. At a certain time in the book Hal encounters two very large lions at night in a park. At first he is terrified but then he realizes that the lions will not attack and moves on. This has changed humanity all together, one article Hal observed had a meaningful quote in it; "they took the man out of man." That quote basically sums it up. Later, while Hal is at his resort, he begins to think about why people are even living anymore. He starts having thoughts about existentialism and nihilism. He tries to explain to himself why mankind has stopped to wonder or explore. Thoughts arise about what he has to live for and if he should do anything about his situation. Even with his wife Eri he feels like a strange foreigner. All these thoughts packed into one book provide one fantastic story.

When Hal Bregg left Earth, he believed that he was doing something great for mankind and that he was going to be remembered for all time. Throughout his missions he became more and more lonely and depressed. There were so many ways to die in space and the odds of one of those things happening was not that small, as he found out when about half of his crew died. One died in a probe sent out to gather data on a planet, and Hal waited all alone for his crew-mate for more than two days even though he knew there was almost no chance of him being found. Another died on a planetoid, and when Hal went down onto the surface to find him, he discovered that he was still alive and thought that he was in hell. Hal was shot in the stomach trying to take his crew-mate back to the main ship. Others died as well, and when Hal returned to Earth, he was hardly recognized for his efforts and deeds. No one cared anymore. Since space exploration was deemed useless, society only noticed that a large old man was now walking the streets, and not a space hero that had returned from the stars. Since space travel can never be any

faster than the speed of light, it was found that any attempt to find intelligent life forms was

pointless. It was never scientifically proven in the story that faster-than-light travel existed. The

only proof was that if an alien civilization discovered this technology of faster-than-light travel

they would eventually come to our universe or within our range of vision, and since that has

never happened in recorded history, it is highly unlikely that it exists at all. Also, since the time

difference between the explorer and Earth was so great, it would be worthless to send out an

expedition that would take 200 years to return from. These are just some of the views on space

travel and humanity that I received from reading this book, but there are several more.

I recommend this book to anyone who likes to think deeper than the every-day things like

soap operas and what is "hip" in fashion. If you have never read science fiction before, I

recommend this book to you. It gives you a chance to escape this world and enter an entirely

new one. Some of the stereotypes of science fiction repulse people away from any good worth

while science fiction novels. Do not believe that all science fiction is Star Trek and Star Wars

where every character has some long unpronounceable name from a planet far, far away and a

time long, long ago. That would be like believing the only romantic thing every written was

Romeo and Juliet. Out of all the great novels on the list I received to choose from, this one was

not even on it. Another book by the same author called Solaris was, though. I read a few

reviews on this book and found that it did not seem like I would enjoy it. The library had this

book so I checked this out instead and my teacher okayed it. I strongly urge that this book be put

on the list of great novels. I have also read Papillon and All Quite On the Western Front, and

this book, in my mind, is the best of the three. So, in conclusion, I recommend this book to

anyone who likes to read and think.

Papillon is one of the best novels I have ever read. And I have read many good novels. Written by Henri Charriere, he tells of his years in the French penal colonies in the northern part of the French Guiana, which is directly north of Brazil. The time frame of the novel is the 30s and 40s. Papillon was sent to hard labor for life after he was convicted of killing a man. Although he says he is innocent, the jury found him guilty without any true physical evidence. Throughout his first few weeks of his prison life, all he could think about was how to get his revenge on the jury, the prosecutor, and the judge. However, as the months passed by, he was convinced that he must escape. With the help of some of his closest friends and a few outside connections, he made an escape only 42 days after his arrival in prison. Throughout his first cavale (or escape, as we would call it), he encounters many problems. For example his boat turns out to be worthless, or they don't have the proper sailing supplies, and many other problems. However, many of the strangers help out Papillon and his fellow escapees. This is one of the most surprising aspects of this novel, the hospitality shown by these complete strangers when they know that they are helping escaped convicts. Papillon is eventually caught and sent to solitary confinement for two years. After many more escape attempts and more years in prison and solitary confinement, he is sent to an island where the prisoners are allowed to live in their own huts and garden and do as they please all day long. Papillon finally escaped from this island by using a coconut raft and after days of floating in the sun, he reaches freedom. The theme of hospitality in this novel is astonishing. These people knew what would happen if they were caught helping the fugitives, but they still gave them advice, directions, clothes, food, shelter, cigarettes (which was one of the few pleasures of prisoners), and many other useful items.

The first man Papillon came across after his escape from Saint Laurent du Marr-On-ee was a woodsman named Brenton. Papillon and his 2 friends, Clousiot and Maturette were waiting in the brush for their other escapees to come with supplies for their boat. One of the days Papillon was found by Brenton, who instead of turning the convicts or even shooting them on the spot, he helped them out. He wanted to see that they had a safe journey to freedom and that their boat was sea worthy. The Brenton gave them detailed directions to an island in order to get a better boat, he gave them one of his boats, and didn't even ask for anything at all in return. To me this is on of the best examples of kindness and concern for a fellow man in need. The Brenton could have shot the 3 men on the spot because he was out hunting for birds, or he could have turned them into the police where they would have faced either death or severe punishment. It was hard to believe that a man living alone in the wooded area next to a French penal colony would be so willing to help 3 dangerous criminals. After the Brenton sent them off to find a new boat for their journey to safety, he mentioned that the island that they would be going to ("Ile aux Pigeons") is inhabited by lepers. Leprosy is a devastating disease that cause the body to literally fall apart. It is contagious only by touch so the French send all criminals who have the disease to this island. Once Papillon arrived at the island, he was greeted with a welcoming hand…so to speak. The lepers could not believe that a man would come to the island voluntarily for any reason at all. Papillon and the leader of the lepers discussed the matter about getting a new boat, and agreed on a deal. The lepers then retrieved a very nice boat, and spent days fixing it for the fugitives. All the while the lepers invited them in for food and shelter. The lepers have separate eating bowls and plates for the few travelers they receive. Then, after the boat was ready for departure, the lepers gave…GAVE the 3 men a large amount of money, rum, tobacco, and many other very useful items to be used on the trip. They lepers explained that they hardly ever use money and that they would be happy to lend a hand to escaped convicts. Papillon was without words as the lepers displayed this amazing show of kindness. And myself, I could not believe that these men, some without a face or hands or feet, gave so much to three strangers. And the fact that they cared for Papillon and his friends, they made sure that they didn't get infected or have any troubles during their stay. This was one of the most surprising displays of human concern in the entire novel. It was great to see men from totally different communities and backgrounds helping out three escaped criminals to get to freedom. And only for a small amount of money. The generosity by the lepers was almost indescribable by Papillon. If it wasn't for the lepers, Papillon and his friends would never had made it as far as they did on their first escape attempt. The last display of hospitality and generosity that I choose to discuss is when Papillon and his friends landed at Trinidad and met a wealthy English family. The law in Trinidad is that escaped prisoners would be sent back to prison in about a week if they choose to stay in Trinidad. The family that the three came across was more than happy to invite them into their home and let them stay for days. This family of 3 let the prisoners shower, shave, get brand new clean clothes, eat as much food as they wanted, stay in the house, get medical treatment, and just about any other thing imaginable. It was as if the prisoners were relatives staying for a few days. That is how well they were treated. The daughter of the English couple was fascinated by the prisoners and talked to them for hours about their adventures. Then, something happened that shocked Papillon completely. The man of the house, Mr. Bowen, left for an entire day. Leaving his wife and daughter alone with Papillon and his friends. That man put enough trust into Papillon to leave his house and family with him! This was so amazing for Papillon he couldn't think of what to do in return for all of his hospitality. The groups talked for days, ate together, and shared stories together. Upon Papillon's departure, the daughter gave him the address of the house, asking him to write them back sometime to let them know if they made it to freedom. Time after time, Papillon was astonished by how much these total strangers cared about another's life and freedom. He only wished someday he could return the favor to the Brenton, the lepers, and the Bowen family.

In conclusion, the theme of hospitality, generosity, and care for fellow man is one of the most outstanding themes in this novel by Henri Charriere. Henri Charriere is probably one of the few people living that have seen human nature at its best. With his encounter with the Brenton in the wooded marshy area, or his stay at the leper island, or his visit at the Bowen house in Trinidad, he has seen more kindness and caring then most people will see their whole lives. If only everyone could have the chance to experience what Papillon experienced. This novel is probably my favorite book to read, not only because its display of human nature, but its display of what prison is like in the French penal colonies, and what it was like to fear for your life every day from fellow inmates and even guards. This novel, I believe, should be required reading material for all students. Its just that good.

Eric Harris
period 5, 8/19/98
Webb

Great Senior Expectations

At last, the last year of my high school education has come. I will experience several new subjects, review several old ones, and no doubt learn many new and useful things that will help me in life. In general, I am expecting to learn to express my opinions and beliefs in a civilized, respectable manner. I expect to learn about people around me, how they act, and their beliefs along with learning to respect their opinions. I also am expecting to learn more about how to be a successful and respectable leader and to become responsible.

Learning to express opinons in a civilized manner is very important in the "real world." One cannot make a difference if one cannot express opinions properly. With the classes I am scheduled to take, I am expecting to learn how to do so. I want to learn how to form and record opinions and use references, statistics, quotations, and other useful ways to get my points across. I expect to learn as much as I can from my Writers Inc. book and learn to apply it to my work. This will all be very important for any college I choose to go to, if I choose to go at all. These skills will help me achieve higher scores on essays and will help me learn more about my topics. There is really no way that this will not benefit me, no matter if I go to Harvard or if I travel the world.

Different people influence my life in different ways. Therefore it is important to learn how exactly they influence me and my decisions, along with how they think and how they form their own decisions. It will also be helpful to learn how people think and why they act the way they do. This skill could help out in almost any line of work and in every day life as well. Learning of peoples' beliefs and religions is also important. It is a good value to respect everyone for who they are and for what they believe in, instead of having stereotypes and

Eric Harris
period 5, 8/19/98
Webb

prejudiced views. Although this may be hard for some people, and even for me, I am expecting

to learn how to do these things in the senior year.

Being a leader is a very admirable quality. I respect people who are good strong leaders

and know what they are doing, and I do not respect people who are weak, uneducated leaders.

This is why I want to be a strong leader. I am hoping team sports and other classes will help me

achieve this quality. If I am considering a military career, then leadership is an extremely

important quality. I am expecting to learn how to be organized and responsible, how to treat

people equally, how to listen attentively and how to solve problems logically. I am hoping my

senior classes and experiences will help my goals.

In conclusion, I expect my senior year to be full of surprises. On the other hand, I want to

achieve certain goals so I am a better person once I graduate. I am expecting to learn how to

express my beliefs and opinions in a civilized, respectable manner, to learn to respect people

around me along with their opinoins and beliefs, to learn how others think and why they think

that way, and to be a strong responsible leader. I believe with the classes I will take and the

opportunities I will have, these expectations will indeed be met.

✓

25 things that make me different

1 My love for a computer game called DOOM. Doom is such a big part of my life and no one I know can recreate environments in Doom as good as me. I know almost anything there is to know about that game, so I believe that seperates me from the rest of the world.

2 My dreams; Dreams are one of the most personal things for a person, and I know my dreams seperate me from others.

3 My car! no one else except my best friend has a little puny car with a RAMMSTEIN sticker on it.

4 My bullet ~~hanging~~ hanging from my rear-view mirror.

5 my berserk and zippo that I always have in ~~a~~ my right pocket.

6 my backpack. With its customized white out wrightings.

7 I can bite off part of a pop can. ~~the~~ using only my teeth.

8 My personal views of other people.

9 My first impressions of people.

10 my penmanship. I haven't seen anyone else write ~~~~ either quite like I do.

11 my knowledge of fireworks

12 my ~~~~ knowledge of ~~~~ conventional/amature explosives.

13 My scars.

14 My anger managment problems.

15 my attitude towards people around me.

16 My diversion record.

17 My friends.

? My patented way of killing spiders and crickets

My nickname, just as long as there isn't too many copy cats out there ?

106

20 My music.
21 My fence signs in my room.
22 the large collection of bullet shells I have.
23 My black box and it's contents
24 My family
25 My memories of the past and hopes for the future

25 ~~25~~ 1 most important thing

Doom is so burned into my head my thoughts ~~usally~~ usually have something to do with the game. Whether it be a level or environment or whatever. In fact a dream I had yesterday was about a "Deathmatch" level that I have never even been to. It was so vivid and detailed I will probably try to recreate it using a map editor. It had 3 ledges and a very high tree-house like area also. but describing it would take forever. What I cant do in real life, I try to do in doom. like if I walk by a small building I would recreate it as good as I could and then explore it. go on the roof, under it, or even shoot at it. The fact is, I love that game and if others tell me "hey its just a game" I say "ok, I dont care"

Music, the music I listen to is fairly unique. However, one must remember that in this day and age, it is almost impossible to be original, so I try to be as much as I can, but I always see someone doing what I do except doing a worse job. I like RAMMSTEIN, KMFDM, 242, ORBITAL, and Lorena McKennitt. So mostly techno/industrial or trance music. I like RAMMSTEIN because they are a german band. Since I am learning to speak German, I know what they are saying. KMFDM is a favorite of mine because of the points they are trying to get across. I'm sure there are others who like my music, but hey, I dont care just as long as they respect the bands.

Accomplishment ✓

A struggle that I had not too long ago was doing community service. I needed to complete 45 hours of comm. serv. by August 3, starting in June. It was part of my Diversion contract, so if I didn't complete it in time, it would be very bad news for Yours Truly. I decided to do my hours at a recreation center called "The Link". It wasn't too hard or harsh, mostly picking up trash or sweeping. Once August 3 rolled around I can note a few problems. I was scheduled to finish my last 4 hours that day (8/3/) except that morning I discovered a rather large nail in my left rear tire. That delayed me about 45 min. I showed up at the Link at 2:00 and the 2 men I had been working under, all the other days, were out of town until Monday morning. Plus, since I didn't know the place closed at 4 on Sundays, that news didn't help much. The man there was nice enough to slide me the extra hours since I did such an outstanding job. So I ended up going back to the Link the next morning to get the final hours-slip signed by the head boss there, and then to go pick up my fixed flat tire and then I was off to Golden to see my diversion officer. With all 45 hours done, It made me feel proud of myself for blowing past all problems and getting it all taken care of.

Eric Harris
Period 2
8/28/98

A recent article in the <u>Rocky Mountain News</u> talked about how an "entire generation is on trial." Bill Clinton and Monica Lewinsky, Kenneth Starr, Susan McDougal, and several powerful leaders in the past were all mentioned. The author talked about how the public does not understand the society in which it lives. He talked about how the public is manipulated and brainwashed into having bogus opinions about others in the news. "How come the public has a more negative view of Monica Lewinsky than Bill Clinton? It takes two to tango so why is Monica more to blame than Bill?" is one view he had. He also explained how people in the past such as Hitler and Evita got the power and love of their people by hardly doing anything to deserve it. The author suggests interviewing an interviewer whose integrity is respected and whose style is to bring out what the guest has to say, rather than impose his own agenda on the discussion. He believes that if the public still doesn't understand issues after seeing both sides of the story, then we should being to give up hope.

I agree with this author. I believe he has several very interesting points and comments. The public can indeed be misled to believe things that it would normally find "wrong" or "immoral." I believe that more and more people in this day and age are becoming, or at least think they are becoming, less attentive and caring less about media and politics. More people think they "don't care" about things like the Lewinsky story or about O.J. Simpson or stories like those, but they still watch the news reports on them, and they still buy articles and magazines that contradict what they say. Not everyone is like that, so I am not saying everyone is a hypocrite. However, I think that if the news reports and magazine articles keep filling people's minds with certain points of views, then eventually those people will start to think that way, as the author of the above article mentioned.

Picture an Earth that has been obliterated by nuclear war and alien attacks leaving cities and military forces in ruins with only a lone marine as humanity's last fighting force. Picture holographic walls, crushing ceilings, oceans of blood and lava, strange ancient artifacts, and horrible sour lemon and rotten meat stenches in the air. Imagine being trapped on an abandoned cold steel base floating in space for eternity, a leathery skinned monster roaming under a strobe light waiting for a fight, and astonishing weaponry designed to your special needs. All these places and ideas have been created and recreated many times by yours truly.

It can be hard to be original in our generation, with so many movies, books, published ideas, and songs that can copied. People can combine ideas from several different fields and mix them into a new trend or fashion but, in reality, it is just more of the same. In order to tell of my creative talents, I must first tell my view on "creativity." My mind is so full of creative, original ideas that sometimes I have trouble keeping them at bay. For the past three years, I have been involved in a computer game called Doom. Even though one might think it is just a game, I believe it is one of the best ways to show my creativity and intelligence.

I believe creativity is a term that is relative to the observer. What one person may think is completely incredible and uncanny, another might think is just more of the same. In reality they both can be correct. I think that about a third of what an average high school student says in one day can be found in a movie or a book. While that student may not be plagiarizing on purpose, someone else might think they are. My point is that, for me, it is hard to describe my creative talents and to be sure that they are original and unique at the same time.

Eric Harris
Period 5, 8/31/98
Webb

Doom is a first-person "shoot-em-up" style game. So basically, one runs around levels and shoots at monsters with military weaponry. To most people it may be just another silly computer game, but to me it is an outlet for my thoughts and dreams. I have mastered changing anything that is possible to change in that game, such as the speed of weapons, the strength and mass of monsters, the textures and colors used on the floors and walls, and greatest of all, the actual levels that are used. Several times I have dreamed of a place or area one night, and then thought about it for days and days. Then, I would recreate it in Doom using everything from places in outer space with burned-out floor lights and dusty computers to the darkest depths of the infernal regions with minotaurs and demons running at me from every dark and threatening corner. I have also created settings such as eras of ancient abandoned military installations deep in monster-infested forests with blood stained trees and unidentifiable mangled bodies covered with dead vines and others that portray to futuristic military bases on Mars overrun with zombies that lurk in every corner. These places may seem a bit on the violent side and, I assure you, some of them are. However, many times I have made levels with absolutely no monsters or guns in them. I have created worlds with beautiful, breath taking scenery that looks like something out of a science fiction movie, a fantasy movie, or even some "eldritch" from H. P. Lovecraft.

Now, I know that other people are just as creative or more creative than I am, but I believe that I will always be the best at Doom creativity. In this day and age it can be hard to find a skill that can be completely dominated and mastered or a skill that almost no one else has. This is why I choose a simple computer game to express my talents.

Is murder or breaking the ✓ 9/2
law ever justified? Explain.

Yes it is. in extreme situations crimes can be
deemed insignificant. For example, say John is holding
Jill hostage and is threatening to blow up her,
himself and a bunch of people. He starts a timer
that can't be stopped and then a police sniper fires
and kills John. now, murdering John is technically
a crime but if he wasn't taken out then lots
of people would have died. Another example is. Say
someone is holding your pet hostage and if you
call for help the pet will die. The terrorist tells
you to go steal a car for him without contacting
anyone for help, I believe in that case grand
theft auto is justified. So if the life of many or
even one human or even animal is at stake and it
is an extreme situation, then breaking the law can
be justified. It all depends on the situation
there can be several different factors that can all change
how the situation is, so I don't think one can
say "NO" to the question. There is always an exception

Eric Harris
Period 2
9/11/98

The article I chose to review this week is an article on daytime napping. The author reviewed a book on the art of napping. It is suggested that a 15 to 20 minute nap during the early afternoon can be beneficial. Any more could be considered as sleep inertia. Creativity and problem-solving skills can be regained by taking a short nap. One professor says that approximately eight hours after you awake you can experience a large drop in alertness. The author reviewed one company who decided to incorporate a nap-room into their daily routine. Employees can sign-up for naps during the day and not have to worry about getting in trouble with their boss.

Personally I agree with the author and the professor mentioned above. About eight hours after I wake up I get very sleepy and I become less and less alert. That, although, is on an average, uneventful day. Now I am not saying that Columbine should throw in a few "nap-hours" around lunchtime, but it might not hurt. Going to bed earlier could help too, but I believe it's harder to go to bed earlier than it is to take a nap later. Some people may say we are just lazy, and they might be right, but if we are lazy and not hurting anyone then what is the loss? If I have two hours to get a job done and I can finish it in one, why not sleep? It can be brought down into an ethical/moral question and argued out even more, but I think if you want to sleep, go ahead. Just don't get in the way.

open Topic ✓

anything huh. Well let me think here. How about a train of thought type writing. Maybe, oh I know, I needed to think about my latest Doom 2 level. It's called Tier 6 and, obviously, is the 6th level in this series. I have trouble making this one for some reason though. In the past I have been able to just go a create several rooms and hallways and secret rooms just off the kopf. but for some reason I cant for Tier 6. Maybe its the fact that school is back in session and there is more on my mind now than there was during the summer when 1-5 were made. I ~~keep~~ keep making just plain, boring, empty rooms like I am a beginner. Just room after room of the same old stuff. There are a few places that are indeed good, quality areas that look better than the original game, but I need to have the whole level like that. I am trying to go for a very tough, action-packed, fast-pace, level because I just saw "Saving Pvt. Ryan" again and I want to kind of recreate some of those scenes best I can. Its tough though... (no more time)

I had a dream a few nights ago. So I will tell
of it. I was walking down a tunnel with a squad
of marines. I recognized 3 of my friends and the rest
of the squad were just ~~enormous~~ soldiers. we were
all armed and we were on some kind of patrol
looking for aliens (like from the movie ALIENS). Then.
bullets started coming from down the tunnel and
hitting the marines in the front. The tunnel was
20 feet wide and high, with a damp, musty, dark feeling
to it ... (no more time)

Good to be bad, bad to be good ✓

A time when it was bad to be good was when I had to give away all my weapons to my parents. It was after I got into serious trouble with the law, so my parents wanted to take all forms of weapons that I had away. It was bad not because I might use the weapons, just because I paid good money or spent a lot of time making them. It made me feel that all that time and money was wasted. But since weapons are dangerous and my parents didn't trust me, I suppose it was for the better.

Eric Harris
Period 2
9/25/98

The article I reviewed this week was an editorial from a local newspaper. The author discussed how Americans are open to talk about almost anything, except death. He says that 81% of Americans have not talked with their doctors about the medical issues of dying. Also, patients that are terminally ill are reluctant to talk about death with their family members and their families are even reluctant to carry out their final wishes. Very few Americans take advantage of federal laws that allow them to determine the nature of the care they will get in their dying hours.

My response to this article is that I think that more Americans need to discuss death with their families and with their doctors. It is a fact of life, and it seems in this day and age people talk about just about anything they can think up. From sexual situations to violence on the streets to alien encounters, we talk about it all. So why not death? Perhaps with today's technology we receive a false sense of security in the fact that we think we could die the next day. With medical technology and thousands of safety procedures in today's society, I believe that the majority of the people think, "oh I'll talk about death some other time, it's not like I'll be dying soon." It may be a hard topic, but oh well, it definitely needs to be discussed incase of the terrible event that a loved one slips into a coma or something of that nature.

Spit vs. Kiss ✓   9/29/98

It is "sick" because it is only a different way of
doing practically the same thing. Kissing is a sign
of affection, therefor it is socially acceptable. It
has emotional values and it can mean several things,
where as swapping spit is just plain, cut, and easily
defined. It has no emotional or spiritual meaning.
personally I think both actions are the same

Nature is evil in Macbeth.

Eric Harris

9/29/98

period 5

Webb

(IV.i.48) implies that the witches are representing darkness and evil. Nighttime and darkness are common symbols of things that are bad or unnatural. These quotations show that Shakespeare, using witches, exercised the use of nature as forces of evil in his play several times.

The murder of Banquo in the third act uses nature as a force of evil in several different ways. "The west yet glimmers with some streaks of day," (III.iii.8) is one such example. This quotation implies that the sun will soon be down and darkness will come over the land. Banquo is approaching into the murderers' trap and therefor darkness is being used as an evil setting. Since Banquo is murdered in the dark, darkness can be said to be evil. When Banquo says, "Give us a light there, ho!" (III.iii.12) he is calling to his murderers, which shows a bit of dramatic irony. The murders give him a false sense of security by showing him light to guide him into their trap. Therefor, in this case, light is used as an evil force of nature. Banquo practically helps call the murderers upon himself when he says, "It will be rain tonight," (III.iii.23) since rain is an unnatural event in nature. Banquo is about to be murdered when he says this, and rain is an unnatural event, so therefor rain is used for an evil force of nature. During the murder the one light is blown out, once again proving that darkness is an evil force of nature. The act of murdering is evil and definitely unnatural, and a murder in the dark is just that much more evil. Banquo's murder has several evil forces of nature surrounding it, such as darkness and nighttime. This proves that nature is used as a force of evil in the play.

Nature is a popular theme in many stories and plays. William Shakespeare is one master at using this theme to his advantage. In his play, Macbeth, nature is used as a force of evil. Throughout the play darkness, nighttime, witches, thunder, and lightning are used as forces of evil. Witches represent the unnatural and chaotic side of nature along with pure evil. The murder of Banquo proves that darkness and nighttime are used as forces of evil and that bad things occur during these time periods or locations. The use of nature as a force of evil is definitely obvious in the play, Macbeth.

This week's article was on a bill recently rejected in Erie, Indiana. The bill was to have every homeowner in the town to own a firearm, and to have it in working condition in his/her household. The bill was rejected and was considered too dangerous. Arguments were that in cities with the strictest gun laws, gun crimes were the highest. So therefor, if gun laws were diminished in severity, and homeowners had guns, the crime rate would go down.

My response to this article is that I think in theory the bill was a good idea. Having a gun in every house would most definitely decrease crime. However, since not every homeowner is all that responsible, intelligent, and wise, other problems would arise. Children playing with loaded weapons and getting hurt, normal household disputes are solved with gunfire, accidental shootings would rise and rise. I believe that it is a law of nature that not everything can work smoothly and turn out the way it was supposed to. While crimes like burglaries and robberies would go down, shootings would most likely skyrocket. So therefor I think it was a good idea to reject this bill.

From this poem I see an image of dead
soldiers in a field. The field is peaceful and green
with small "poppies" in it. But then I see a soldier
holding a flag. As that soldier falls another
comes up and takes the flag and holds it up
high. The fallen soldiers want the living ones
to keep faith in what they are fighting for and
to keep on fighting. The dead are sad that they
died, they miss the sunsets, the dawn, and
love. However, the soldiers have escaped the guns
of battle judging from what the 1st verse says,
"The larks... guns below."

The song deadens the meaning of the
poem. It changed into some shallow meaningless
song with words ~~when~~ it was ~~~~ a good
poem. That's really about all I ~~can~~ ~~~~ write
about it.

My article review this week is about an article in which the author describes how dropping bombs and missiles are cowardly, indiscriminate, and a little short of terrorism. The author used a scene from Saving Private Ryan in which an American fighter plane bombs a tank right in front of Tom Hanks. The author said that even with today's weapons that is hard to do. He also describes how the public feels about bombs and missiles. He says that the public likes "clean" air campaigns and watching the little TV video of a building blowing up in the desert. His basic point was that the bombers and fighters in the air was and is not the only way to win, that it still counts on the soldiers on the ground.

My response to this article is that I think this person has never really paid much attention to how violence and wars work. In regards to his first comment, that scene in Saving Private Ryan where the tank is destroyed is most definitely possible and happened many times over the course of the war, that's why the planes were called "tank busters." Who ever said launching missiles was courageous? I know I sure didn't and I believe our generals didn't either. It is simply a much better way to solve problems and to eliminate installations than sending in an entire battalion. Of course wars still rely on the ground troops, but air support is definitely a part of winning the war. The author says, "How noble is a cause worthy only of having your bombs thrown into it, and not your sons?" Sending your sons off to fight and die for your country is one thing, but the simple act of pushing a button is another. Usually, if bombs and cruise missiles can't stop the enemy, then we send in the ground troops. Of course a fighter plane isn't enough, but neither is the ground force.

"Trying to define yourself is like trying to bite your own teeth." I interpret this to mean that you can't define yourself. no matter how hard you try or for how long, it is impossible. This is most definitely true. ~~because~~ Personally I have been trying to define who I am, to put myself under some sort of catagory, to ~~to the~~ somehow help myself understand who ~~I~~ I am and what I stand for. It seems like every week my point of view changes on people, but yet it stays the same. What a paradox huh. Minds change constantly, whenever I try to figure something out that means something to me I can never come up with an exact conclusion. There is always exceptions and stuff. I don't think humans are meant to define themselves, we just make quick judgements and go with that, sometimes we will spend an entire lifetime trying to figure out someone and even after that ~~long~~ length of time we still can't possibly know everything about that person. The same goes for ourselves, just when we think we know who we are when a new event happens that throws everything we knew about ourselves out the window.

whats 35% of 100 ✓

10/13/98

1. 35
2. Germany France Spain Italy
3. Kansas Wyoming Nebraska Arizona

I think that this is absolutely ridiculous. people who can't answer questions like that should be shot. The schools are so caught up on trying to educate students on worthless subjects that they forget about the basics. now usually for most schools that isn't the case, but if it is for even 1 shool thats a big problem. I think students today are astonishingly stupid. It never ceases to amaze me how stupid and ignorant people can be. Seems like some try to be dumb. Its a pity natural selection doesn't apply to humans, otherwise I strongly beleive the race as a whole would be better off. I am ashamed to be a part of the same species as some of these people. and to think that this is what millions of soldiers died for and risked everything they had for back in WWII and korea and vietnam. and now there are students who don't even know who was involved in the first world war or don't even know when the first atomic bomb was dropped. its is truely pitifull

~~There is it so soon~~ There is no reality except
the one contained within us. That is why so
many people live such an unreal life. They
take the images outside them for reality and
never allow the world within to assert
itself.

I think this is definitely a very true quote.
I think it means that people take in images
that the see for reality and take what they see
in their mind to mean nothing. Except I don't
think that is entirely true, people do act on and
believe in what they see, but they are still
influenced by others. I think people look at others
and think that is what they "have" to be like and
so they aren't who they are on the outside than
on the inside. People also think that whatever
they know and believe in is the only truth, so
when something that goes against the grain happens
they think it is unreal or can't be happening. I
think if more people would let the reality inside
themselves come out it would be a different world.
right now people just think "hey it looks cool
to have a strong opinion on something or to believe
in something, I think I'll do that too" so they gather
up whatever they like about things and try to form
a personality out of it, When they should be doing
whatever they feel like doing on the inside. If that person
wants to be just like everyone else or try to be different
just to be different, then OK. If they want to try
to fly off a bridge, OK. If they want to commit crimes, OK.

This female, who I will call Betsy, is a sad woman. She spends all of her time in front of a mirror putting make-up on. She seems like a slutty, trendy bitch that people like to look at since she seems "pretty" by the social standards. She feels very dense, she just smiles and says "gosh, OK!" in a cheerful but dumb manner. She just wants to be liked. She doesn't know she is different, she thinks she is normal and not different. Some words that would describe her are dense, stupid, shallow, and dazed. She feels happy yet uncomfortable. She is covered with pasty-tan make-up and has golden hair. She smells of cheap perfume and hairspray. I hear wind…or the ocean…when looking at her. She remembers that she has an audition coming up for a cheap B-movie part where she thinks she will be acting. She feels smooth yet cold. The taste of polyester comes to mind.

1. The forest-green field was hot under the sun.
2. The game was in it's 2nd overtime.
3. 5 soccer balls were already destroyed from heavy hits.
4. Injured players were being treated on the side line.
5. ~~Orders~~ Orders that were being yelled by coaches and players
6. Confused us all.
7. Time was running low, as was our energy.
8. The ball must go through the enemy lines.
9. Overhead we saw planes flying by.
10. All in our direction, seeming to give us more power.
11. Their defense was strong.
12. None of our attacks could punch through.
13. We tried several different kinds of attacks,
14. Through pure luck, as always, we made it through.
15. The defenses were smashed and we punched through to the goal
16. As we celebraited our victory, we felt sorry for the other team.
17. But that was just to bad for them.

I think people should learn more about what they are listening to. They need/should actually HEAR what they are listening to every day. People generally listen to music because it "sounds" good. Not many people listen to songs for the lyrics. I think that people should, the band took time to write the song, not just the instrumental part, but the lyric part to. I hear people say things like "Yeah that band rules" or "I love that band their music is so cool!" and they can't even understand what the group is actually talking about. Songs from bands like RAMMSTEIN, KMFDM, NIN, M.M., and more popular ones like the bands played a lot on the radio. People could at least hop on the web and look at the song lyrics or find an English translation so they know what the band is saying, or maybe ask someone who is a big fan and who knows what the band is saying. It's not that hard, and I think it will cut down on a lot of the people in this society that are shallow and naïve who just look at the front cover of the book, and not the pages…to twist around that quote a little.

stupid fucking saxiphone crap. I hate this kinda fuckin
music. Goddamn white bushey apes and spear chuckers
snappin their gay little fingers and tapping their faggot little
shoes. I want to take that sax and toss it into a vat of molten
steel along with it's owner. or maybe charge into their gay little
night club blasting away with an AR15 and kill everyone of those
punkass happy jazzy fuck sticks.

Oh jesus this is even worse than the last piece. This is what
passes for music these days? Buddah, I could go get a music contract.
what catagory is this BS anyway? Shell blowing - bone wacking
Tree shaking Jazz? I really dont want to hear about
some annoying middleaged loser whining about
his stuped stream of consciousness type lyrics.
Next they will throw in some frogs croaching or
chainsaws roaring.

Hmm, a bit calmer so far. no jungle bunnies running around
banging on things. Is this a fast pace song for the Earth spirit
club maybe? Thank God there arent any lyrics. I find
that lyrics can often ruin good music. well this isnt so bad,
kind of trancey. Quick too. was that a dog. Oh goodie, I hear
space invaders now. Damn it, more random crap.
Jesus now its ruined. stupid symbols or whatever they are
called. must be hard to carry tHAT beat. OK now stop screwin
with it.

Oh yip-ee. Enya wannobes with a twist of 80's synthasizer
in it. Now weare a jammin dude. Ug I need some KMFDM.
Is this the soundtrack to a little fantasy movie about a boy
and his star ship cruiser? Sounds like something aerobics
classes dance to when they forget their CDs. hmm, for
some reason I feel like flying through a city with the spice girls.

Ug. This is undescribable I feel like I'm walking around in a friggin cartoon for Gods sakes. Bloody bounto boys and their little banjo barakas. what the fuck is this! Screw you guys, I'm going to lunch. and listening to good fucking music.

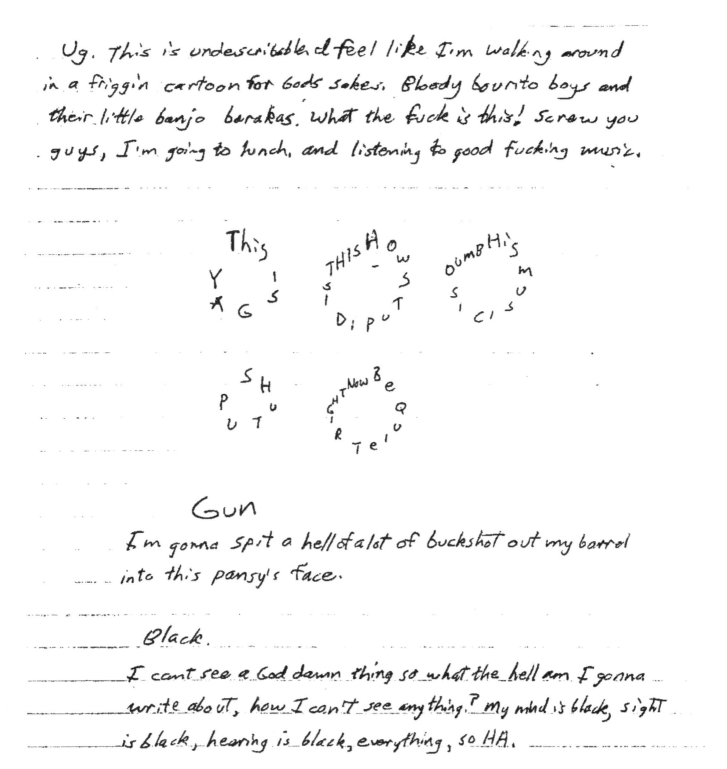

Gun

I'm gonna spit a hell of a lot of buckshot out my barrel into this pansy's face.

Black.

I cant see a God damn thing so what the hell am I gonna write about, how I can't see anything? My mind is black, sight is black, hearing is black, everything, so HA.

Hicks V. Taggart

Age   1 week.
family   OO buck. #7-9 buckshot, slugs.
wish   to kill
fear   water
location Box w/ its brothers
sig. other shotgun.

"I was trying to be loaded into the shotgun when I got jammed in the chamber. The shotgun thought I was all the way in, and tried to fire. IT was to smart for itself because it had a safety mechanism that prevented it from firing. I was pissed that he neglected to notice me being stuck and tried to fire. Oh well, those things happen. He eventually had me cleared and reloaded. I still have scratches on my brass from the damn chamber, so a grudge has remained between me and Arlene.

---

earliest memory is hard to visualize, It might not be even true. My mind tends to blend memories together. I do remember the 4th of July when I was 12. I remember riding my bike down a street. I hid in a closet. I hid from everyone when I wanted to be alone. I remember running outside with a lot of other kids and it felt like an invasion a bonfire in a clearing in a private property area. firework smells ████████ I wanted to chain his hyper ass down. I think I had a buzz cut and was real skinny Shit holes
NO FEAR POGS Green day walked burnt stuff.

134

my room, movie tickets, bullet casolings. _____

6th grade school Bus.

Riding home every day. sitting in the back seats
with ▓▓ ▓▓, ▓▓ and others. Talking about guns,
sex, and people. ▓▓ standing up for his mom saying do mamma
likes to others, ▓▓ being goofy talking about his girlfriends
▓▓ being real quiet with his big brown eyes. our ~~seat~~ refuge
from everyone else. where we talked about personal things

Eric Harris
Period 2
11/5/98

The article I chose to review this week is on drivers not moving for emergency vehicles. The article mentioned how emergency response teams have trouble with motorists getting out of their way when going to or coming from a scene of an accident or emergency. Motorists many times just slam on their brakes in the middle of the road, cause other accidents trying to get out of the way, or don't even know there is a emergency vehicle coming because the radio is too loud or they are on a cell-phone. Recently an ambulance was sideswiped by a motorist who didn't even see/hear it coming, the ambulance was carrying a victim of an earlier accident to a hospital, and a second ambulance was called to the scene because of the motorist's careless driving.

My response to this article is that I think it is completely ridiculous that motorists risk the lives of others that are in desperate need of medical attention because of their arrogance. I have seen people who refuse to move out of the way when a fire truck is trying to get by, with lights and sirens on. Some people think they are so important and their destination is of the utmost priority and that nothing better get in their way. Even if 10 children are burning to death or if an elderly man is having a heart attack, that motorist absolutely must get to the grocery store or to the movie theater. Some people don't even know that they are supposed to get out of the way of emergency vehicles when their lights are on and the siren is flashing. Actually, it is the law. One can get a "failure to yield" ticket and possibly loose points on their license for not getting out of the way. It is not a personal choice one makes to get out of the way, it is the law, and yet people still think, "oh they can go around me," or "hey I have the right-of-way here, even if your lights and sirens are on!"

Précis

    Americans are very interested in music, even though many just sit back and listen to it rather than make it themselves. Many reasons, such as laziness, lack of discipline, and ignorance keep ~~our~~ our musical experience is largely receptive and not creative.

The Nazi Culture

by

Eric Harris

Mr. Webb

Composition for the College Bound

November 13, 1998

Nazism was a form of government unlike any other in history. Lead by Adolf Hitler, the Nazis had distinct beliefs and policies, severe racism and hatred, strong, new family values, and plans for future Germany and the world. The Nazi party came to power in the early 1930s, thanks to Adolf Hitler. Hitler was loved and admired by all of his followers. The Nazis derived many symbols from ancient runes and made code names for things like their concentration camps. They also formed several new laws and restrictions. Racist beliefs and violent actions were all part of everyday life in Nazi Germany. Concentration camps killed millions of people using gas chambers and firing squads. The Jewish race was considered inferior, and therefore extremely and harshly discriminated against by law. Family values were encouraged, education was reformed, the women's roles were outlined, the Aryan race was to be the only race, and law controlled breeding. Education was reformed in order to benefit the state, not the individual. The woman's main role was to bear children, cook, and clean. The Aryan race was the only "superior" race, so therefore Hitler wanted Germany to have all Aryan citizens. Only the elite would reproduce and inferior races were restricted from breeding with the superior race. Hitler had several plans for his new Germany, and for the world as well. Hitler wanted leaders in Germany. He also wanted to control what everyone saw and heard to maintain a working state. The youth of the world was to be under Nazi control, and Europe and Russia were to be conquered. Approximately eleven million people died as a result of the Nazis. The Nazis were one of the most racist forms of government ever.

i

Thesis: Nazism was a form of government unlike any other in history, with their beliefs and policies, their racism and hatred, their very strong family values, and the plans they had in store for the rest of the world.

I. The Nazis
    A. How they came to power
        1. Hitler
        2. Love for Hitler
        3. Energy
    B. Who they were
        1. Runes
        2. Code words
    C. Policies
        1. Censorship
        2. Control
        3. Euthanasia
        4. Aliens

II. Racism and violence
    A. Concentration camps
        1. Doctors and wives
        2. Shootings
        3. Gas chambers
        4. Reinforcement of hatred
    B. Jews
        1. Insults and racist comments
        2. Inferior race

III.   Family values
    A. Education
        1. What education would benefit
        2. Textbooks
        3. Science in racism
    B. Women
        1. Children
        2. Discrimination
    C. Aryan race
        1. Mental
        2. Physical
    D. Breeding
        1. Only the elite would reproduce
        2. Jews as inferiors

IV.   Future Plans
    A. Europe
        1. Leaders
        2. Freedoms
        3. Censorship of the nation
    B. World
        1. Youth
        2. Russia
        3. Space

The Nazi Culture

How many people can a football stadium hold? Can it hold fifty, sixty thousand? Most stadiums can. Now, picture a stadium filled, not just seats but the field and all the air above it, with dead men, women, and children. That is just a fraction of the casualties inflicted by the Nazis, also known as the Third Reich. Through the 1920s and 1930s ideas from the past and basically anything that seemed interesting to Adolf Hitler was added into the government policies. Nazism was a form of government unlike any other in history, with their beliefs and policies, their racism and hatred, their very strong family values, and their plans for the rest of the world.

The word "Nazi" itself is synonymous with "racist." The Third Reich, in its early years, was a form of government that was like a magnet, sucking in anything that could build on the racist foundation laid out by Hitler. Theories and policies from the past were resurrected to go alongside the growing power of the nation. A perfect nation was their goal. With Hitler leading the National Socialists, or Nazis, with his astonishing political skills, they adopted symbols from the past and made policies to turn Germany into a National Socialist country.

Some people ask, "How did such an evil empire come to be?" The answer is simple. Germany needed a leader and Hitler was the best leader Germany had. His persuasive, manipulative speeches and his promises for a great nation were enough to get almost the entire German community to strongly support him (Nyomarkey 12). The Germans wanted something to be proud of, and Hitler was able to provide it for them. With Hitler saying things like, "The common interest before self interest," and "Love Germany more than anything, and your fellow Germans more than yourself!" the German people felt like they were part of something special and exciting (Remak 39). His orders, whether written or oral, "cancelled all written law" (Nyomarkey 12). The German people accepted this and loved their leader. They were glad to see Germany being brought out of the economic depression it was in. Germany, under the Nazi regime, was overcoming the effects of the great depression (Remak 75). This boosted the community's moral. Hitler got the Germans moving again and gave them something to strive for. A certain energy, "…a feeling that things were moving again, that a new energy had been infused into German life," as described by one citizen, was moving through Germany (Remak 71). A new social structure was being *good concisent* formed, with Hitler and his ideas at the top.

The Nazis used several ancient runes in their flags and military signs, along with special code words used by officers. The swastika itself, a symbol now imbedded into many minds as a symbol of evil, was derived from an ancient rune known as a *Hakenkreuz*. It was a pagan Germanic symbol of the god of thunder — *really? I didn't know there was a connection* known as Donnor or Thor ("History"). Its red background indicated the "social idea of the movement," and the white circle indicated its "nationalism" (Thornton 25). The Nazi's "SS" symbol was also an ancient pagan rune, known as a *sig-rune*. By *this is interesting* itself the sig-rune was only one large lightning bolt-type "S" which symbolized victory ("History"). A badge manufacturer, who just put two of the *sig-runes* together, invented the "SS" symbol. Code words, such as Aktion T4 and KZ were used often by Nazi officers. Aktion T4 was the code name of the euthanasia program

that led to the killing of approximately 100,000 lives that were "not worth living."
Aktion T4 was named after the relevant government department of the Reich
chancellery located on Tiergarten Strasse 4 in Berlin ("History"). KZ stood for
Konzentrazionslager, which means concentration camp. It was used constantly by
Nazi officers and soldiers to somewhat lessen the idea of the camps, and what they
were used for ("History"). The Third Reich was definitely a unique government,
using symbols from ancient pagan runes and coming up with entirely new and
extremely racist laws.

Racism was rooted into the Nazi government just like freedom is rooted in
America's government. Laws for censorship, foreigners, and duties of citizens were
all intended to protect the state. Hitler once stated that "We have to put a stop to the
idea that it is a part of everybody's civil rights to say what he pleases" (Remak 83).
Strong censorship was imposed in Germany against books, articles, magazines, films,
and even art. Nazi rulers had complete control over what they wanted their citizens to
see, hear, and read. They indeed "...had a free hand to determine[,] if it could, every
man's attitude toward life," (Moose xxi). Euthanasia is a current topic in today's
American society, but in Nazi Germany, all mentally disabled people or "incurable
mental defectives" were killed due to the Aktion T4 project (Thornton 28). A citizen
had strict duties and at the top of their list was working for the good of the state
(Thornton 24). Aliens, on the other hand, were to be discriminated against. The
German people wanted only pure Germans in their country. Any others were to be
"disposed of." Therefore, foreigners had few rights, and Jews in particular were to be

hated (Thornton 24). The concepts of racial superiority, national community, and leadership were most popular in the Nazi's *weltshauung*, or world view.

Hitler made almost everyone in Germany have a sense of national pride. Policies were made to strengthen the pride and weaken resistance. Strong propaganda techniques using intimidating symbols allowed the Nazis to rule in Germany. With Hitler's ideas and the racism involved in the Third Reich, the killing of millions of people from "inferior races" was deemed necessary. The number of deaths the Nazis are responsible for will never be known, however it is believed that from the concentration camps alone, over eleven million people lost their lives. The Third Reich almost completely wiped out the Jewish population in Europe in the late 1930's and early 1940's. Now in our minds, that is utterly inhumane, immoral, and evil, but in the Nazi's minds it was perfectly fine to exterminate an entire race. The majority of the world's population considers the Nazis evil because of the concentration camps and the treatment of the Jewish race.

The Nazis had a distinct hatred for the Jewish race. They wanted the entire race exterminated and the most efficient way of doing this was to make concentration camps. Nazi doctors controlled life and death in most of the concentration camps. Prisoners considered one doctor, Joseph Mengele, as "…a non-human, evil force…the lord of life and death" (Lifton 345). The wife of a high-ranking Nazi officer near Buchenwald was known to have collected "lampshades, book covers, and gloves made of human skin from murdered concentration camp inmates" (Infield 75). In the earlier years, shootings were the more "popular" way of disposing of Jews. The shootings were very secret though, and since almost all "shootings took place beyond

Germany's borders," it was easier to keep shootings out of the news (Remak 154).

Sometimes twisted Nazi officers would line up prisoners and fire a rifle round into the

first just to see how many chests it would go through. As time passed, gas chambers

and crematoriums became responsible for most of the killing. An SS guard once said,

"the killing way easy…they just went in expecting to take showers and instead of

water we turned on poison gas" (Infield 76). Gassing was indeed the most efficient

method. Because of "…occasional emotional difficulties encountered by the

executioners, who might balk at shooting children, for instance, gassing proved by far

the most efficient method," (Remak 158), says an SS guard in regards to gas

chambers. Methods of killing did vary. In a city called Riga convicts were released,

given iron bars, and ordered to kill Jews (Remak 152). The hatred was constantly

reinforced through speeches from people like Hitler and Himmler. Himmler once

said "whether or not 10,000 Russian women collapse from exhaustion while

digging…interests me only in so far as the ditch is completed for Germany,"

("History") which implies that all he cares for, and all he wants everyone else in

Germany to care for, is Germany. Millions of people died as a result of the

concentration camps.

The amount of hatred for the Jewish race was incredible. The Nazi's hatred

"was symbolized for them by the Jews," who very often became targets, scapegoats,

and the usual suspects (Thornton 10). Nazis constantly insulted the Jewish race.

They were not even regarded as human beings, only "an appearance of putrescence"

(Moose 336). It helped them to build the hatred for the Jews. Public speeches like

"the Jew is…a parasite, a sponger…a pernicious bacillus…his presence is also like that of a vampire; for whenever he established himself [,] the people…are bound to be bled to death…" (Thornton 10) were also used to boost the hatred in Germany. It was all part of their beliefs and they saw nothing wrong with it. "The inhuman persecution of the Jews that the Nazis carried out was firmly based on their view of life," and therefore, in their own minds, killing was right (Thornton 5). In order to maintain their government the Jewish race had to be forced out of the picture.

Many people today have a hard time picturing the overall impact of the concentration camps. One of the largest goals of the Third Reich was to destroy the Jewish race, and they almost did. The Nazis killed approximately six million Jews using gas chambers and firing squads. While the "inferior" Jewish race was being exterminated, the "superior" Aryan race was striving to become stronger workers and families. Family values in Nazi Germany were very strong. Germans wanted to keep their families strong, healthy, and active. Education was revised, the woman's role was changed, and the overall Aryan racial elements were outlined in order to have a more perfect, flawless community.

Education was not made to benefit the individual, but to benefit the state. It was very important for Hitler's youth. He wanted the highest task of education to be the preservation, care, and development of the best racial elements (Pine 1). It was also used to make a more perfect generation of Germans, who were strong and prepared to sacrifice and undertake responsibilities towards the nation community (Pine 1). In order to do this, textbooks and schools were reformed. Nazi symbols were often used within domestic themes in order to make them "familiar and more accessible to children" (Pine 2). Swastikas were inserted into books, pictures of

wow — this is scary. we are very susceptible as a species.

Hitler with children were posted in schools, and eventually school children were putting swastikas in their homes (Pine 2). Scientific and arithmetic examples in textbooks also helped the youth with their racial superiority education. Craniology, the study of the skull, was used to distinguish the "inferior" races from the "superior" races (Pine 4). Arithmetic was used to show how "wasteful" the mentally challenged were and how much money could be saved by euthanasia (Pine 5). These ideas were then transferred to German homes where parents could learn about their roles in the *don't transition here* Third Reich.

The woman's role, in particular, was very unique. Throughout time women have tried to be treated as equals to males. Eventually they did win their rights in America, but in Nazi Germany, the women were supposed to be "glad" to stay home and cook and clean all day long. They were to be "beautiful and to bring children into the world" (Moose 41). It was said that motherhood was in the "front rank of patriotic as well as moral virtues" (Schoenbaum 188). Women were required to raise *increase pop.* the children, cook, clean, and look after the house. It was also "good morals for a woman to have several children" (Moose 37). However, they were still discriminated against. Women who had "many miscarriages, or who brought deformed, sick, or sickly children into the world" were considered inferior (Moose 37). They could not join in politics nor serve in the armed forces. This was all part of the "superior" *don't transition at end of PPs* Aryan race and was considered to be the law.

how about reindeer games? (sorry :))

Those of the Aryan race considered themselves to be members of the superior human race. All others were inferior and were constantly criticized. Extreme racism was used to show the Nazi's superiority. The personal characteristics of the Aryan race included honor, courage, love of freedom, and a strong spirit of scientific

research (Thornton 5). Physically, the Aryans were tall, strong, and long-headed.

They had blue eyes and blond hair, with a fair skin complexion (Thornton 5). Many

attempts were made to increase the "pure" German blood population, such as stealing

children who matched the physical requirements of the Aryan race from their homes.

Himmler once responded to a question that asked "How can we be so cruel as to take

a child from its mother," by saying "How much more cruel [is it] to leave a potential

genius with our natural enemy" (Infield 138). The Nazis were very determined in

forming a perfect German nation.

Breeding became a controlled issue in the Third Reich. Only the elite would

reproduce (Pine 1). It became against the law for a pure German person to breed with

someone who was not. The goal was to bring together a high-grade heredity stock

and to eliminate all inferior races from the German people (Moose 35). They

believed that because of inferior races, like the Jews, many true German families

were ruined by the result of only one "low-grade" person coming into the family.

Once again, it was the Jews' fault for Germany's problems.

Family values in Germany were strengthened during the Third Reich.

Education, along with the woman's role, was reformed according to Nazi beliefs.

The Aryan race and breeding guidelines were also outlined as a result of new policies.

Despite these reforms and new policies, the Nazi regime was defeated. Most of the

leaders fought until the end, turning out new plans for the Third Reich. Hitler had

many plans for his nation and the world that he would never see accomplished.

Hitler's main goals were to conquer Europe and form a perfect Aryan nation. A nation would be created that would thrive on National Socialism. Hitler wanted leaders, but he also wanted all of his citizens to feel equal. "No one should think himself superior to his fellow man" and even leaders should be "devoted to service and responsibilities" (Moose xxxvii). He was afraid that "intellectuals would feel superior to others because of their knowledge and thus form a separate group within the people which would be difficult to control" (Moose xxxvii). As Americans, we consider the freedom of the press as a right. Nazis, on the other hand, only allowed the freedom of the press to be permitted "within a framework conducive to the national welfare" (Thornton 24). A "strict censorship" was also placed on the publishing industry (Pine 1). Hitler wanted the people of his nation only to see what he wanted them to see, in order to have them remain loyal to the Third Reich.

Hitler had plans for Europe, as well as the world. A theory the Nazis believed was that "if youth could be captured by their world view, the future was assured" (Moose xxxii). This means the youth of the world would grow up believing in Nazism whether living in Germany or not. A large plan of Hitler's was to conquer Russia and use the land for farming and for more Germans to live on. There were going to be several "population transfers" (Remak 127) in Europe and Asia, because space was needed for the German people. Space was to be made in several ways, such as "low rations, shootings, an expulsions" (Remak 122). The people would be able to live free, just as long as the Germans were their rulers. In case of a revolution, they would "drop a few bombs on their cities and the affair will be over" (Remak 128). Judaism was also to be "destroyed" since they believed it posed an international threat to Germany (Smith 255). This would allow more room for the German people and exterminate the main "inferior" race in Europe. Those types of events show the care, or lack thereof, for the people of other nations besides Germany. Eventually, if Hitler had won the war, the Third Reich would have spanned over the whole globe and tens of millions or more people would have been eliminated.

scary thought

The Third Reich, at its prime, posed a great threat to the well being of all of the European nations and indeed the whole world. Germany would have been a nation in which all citizens were equal, at least all of the Aryan citizens, and anyone who opposed the Nazis would be killed. Nearby lands would have been conquered and the Jewish population would have been even more diminished. Millions more people would have been killed as a result of the "population transfers" the Germans had in store for their conquered territories.

The Third Reich, led by Adolf Hitler, was one of the most evil and racist forms of government ever. The goals of the Third Reich were to make a perfect Aryan nation, destroy the inferior races, and conquer enough land to accommodate the German people. After Hitler came to power he reformed laws, policies, and family values, and set goals for the future of his nation. Reformations of education and of laws allowed the Third Reich to carry on for years. The concentration camps killed millions. The racist views brainwashed the society into believing the Aryans were superior to all other races. They were responsible for the deaths of at least eleven million people. These things were all part of Hitler's master plan of creating a perfect Aryan race to rule Germany.

a bit too repetitive

Works Cited

"History." Online. Available: *(it's ok to split the address line)*

http://www.geocities.com/Vienna/Strasse/8514/history.html. 25 October

1998.

Infield, Glenn B. Secrets of the SS. Stein and Day. Braircliff Manor, NY. 1981.

Lifton, Robert Jay. The Nazi Doctors. Robert Jay Lifton, 1986.

Moose, George L. Nazi Culture. New York: Grosset and Dunlap, 1966.

Nyomarkay. The Nazi Party. University of Minnesota, 1967.

Pine, Lisa. "Nazism in the Classroom". History Today April 1997: 22-28.

Remak, Joseph. The Nazi Years. Prentice-Hall Inc. Englewood Cliffs, NJ. 1969.

Schoenbaum, David. Hitler's Social Revolution. Doubleday Company, Inc., Garden

City, New York, 1966.

Smith, Woodruff D. The Ideological Origins of Nazi Imperialism. New York:

Oxford University Press, 1986.

Thornton, M. J. Nazism. Pergamon Press Ltd., 1966.

Everyday events can change a life significantly and we might not even be aware of it. Everything we do, say, and see and everything others do always will affect us, no matter what we think. Therefore, it is hard to say which event in my life has had the most serious, dramatic change. I do believe what happened on the last Friday night in January 1998 is the most significant event that has changed my life. My friend Dylan and I were driving around that night at about 9:00 PM with nothing to do. We decided to go to the a dirt parking lot off of deer creek canyon road to just kind of "hang out" to kill sometime. We were planning to check out some movies, and go home to my house and just spend the night there, just another weekend night. We arrived there, and there were 2 cars, a large white utility van and a small red truck, already parked there. We were the only ones there so we just walked around, broke some bottles we found there, lit off some fireworks, and just talked. Then we began thinking about breaking into this van. No one was around, we had a clear line of sight to anything coming and going, and the van was stuffed with electronic equipment. We thought there was no way we would get caught, and everything seemed so easy. So we got a rather large rock, broke the window and Dylan started removing items from the van while I waited in my car keeping a look out for incoming cars. After about 10 minutes I said "that's enough, let's go." So we left the scene and went up to an open space in the mountains. We were sure we had gotten away with it all, so we started reviewing what we had stolen. I got out of my car to put something in my trunk when a Jefferson County sheriff shined his rather bright flashlight into my eyes from the other side of my car. Right then I realized what a damn fool I was for what I did. He had been watching us for about 5 minutes, apparently he had seen us far away, parked his car down the road, and walked up behind my car without us noticing him. We told him everything, and we were arrested. We spent that entire night waiting for the cops to finish searching my car, waiting at the station and filling out forms and giving statements to the cops, explaining to my parents what we had done and why, and then going up to Golden to get "booked." After a very unique experience in a real live police station being a real live criminal, I had lots of time to think about what I did. Remorse put it lightly. I spent about 4 hours there, only about 15 minutes of that was I actually doing something, like giving them any and every imaginable way of taking my fingerprints, or taking my picture. Actually, mug shot would be a more appropriate word. I waited for the rest of the time. Their computer chose that moment to break down, so they put me into prison-type bathroom to wait. As I waited, I cried, I hurt, and I felt like hell. We got home at about 4:30 AM that morning. My parents lost all trust in me, and were completely disappointed beyond belief. April is when our court date finally came around, and we were both sentenced to 1 full year of diversion. Which is a lesser charge since we plead guilty to all charges. So, the consequences of that night were; 1

153

year diversion which includes about 350 dollars worth of fines, a total of 4 full days of classes such as anger management and mother against drunk driving, 45 hours of community service, 2 months grounding, 120 dollar fine for getting my car back (it was impounded), and I am seeing a psychologist to help me with my anger problems. I am glad neither of us drink or do drugs, because that would have sky rocketed our already orbit-level consequences. My parents lost all respect and trust in me and I am still slowly regaining it. That experience showed me that no matter what crime you think of committing, you will get caught, that you must, absolutely must, think things through before you act, and that just because you can do something doesn't mean you should. To this day I still do not have a hard realistic reason why we broke into that car, but since we did, we have been set on a track that makes it mandatory for me to be a literal angel until March of '99. So that will hopefully keep me out of any trouble that I would have gotten into my senior year. Personally, I think that whole entire night was enough punishment for me. On the good side, I have had many new experiences that I am sure will help me with life as a result of being on diversion. So all in all, I guess it was a worth while punishment after all.

Eric,
Wow what a way to learn a lesson. I agree that night was enough punishment for you. Still, I am proud of you and the way you have reacted to this situation. We all make mistakes, how we respond to them is what makes us who we are. You have really learned from this and it has changed the way you think. This may be the best lesson you ever learn. I also think you should know that it's not one action that makes a person who they are. I would trust you in a heartbeat. Thanks for letting me read this and for being in my class.

Sincerely,
Tonelli

My last article is on the new Brady bill. The Brady bill that went into affect recently requires all licensed gun deals to have instant background checks from the FBI when selling a firearm of any kind. In theory this was a good idea. This would keep guns out of the hands of people who have felony charges on their police record, dishonorable discharge from the military and illegal immigrants. The background checks will take anywhere from thirty minutes to a few days.

The FBI just shot themselves in the foot. There are a few loopholes in the new Brady bill. The biggest gaping hole is that the background checks are only required for licensed dealers...not private dealers. The number of licensed dealers dropped from 5,011 in 1993 to 1,715 in 1998. Private dealers can sell shotguns and rifles to anyone who is 18 or older, and they can sell handguns to anyone who is 21 or older, without background checks of any kind. Another problem with the bill is that misdemeanor crimes of abuse and violence do not show up, and sometimes police and mental health records aren't put into the FBI's database. Only about 50% of the needed information is there. Therefore 50% of the criminals who want guns have a pretty good chance of getting them from a licensed dealer.

Trenchcoat Mafia

Hit-Men

For Hire

Eric Harris

Period 2

12/10/98

T-dog

Table-of\-Contents

Product Overview

In this city, protection is needed. Day by day people grow more and more agitated with one another and become less understanding and forgiving. Even though programs made by anti-hate groups and police try to keep people from being prejudiced and having stereotypes, most people are still the same.

The so-called "Trench Coat Mafia" is a small group of friends who generally wear dark clothes, military fatigues, and long black dusters. Most people usually just stare and whisper when they see us. We don't mind because we generally don't like people anyway. Now they have reasons to stay clear of us.

MAP

This map depicts our current locations. We are located in a few different houses in the Columbine area, along with a safe location in the mountains. We also have connections with people in Mexico, Germany, South Africa, and New York City. The locations in the Columbine area are strategically positioned so we can launch attacks in almost any neighborhood with a few minutes notice. We also have caches of weaponry and explosives located around the CHS area and in certain fields, all to serve you, the customer.

Business Organization

Now, with more and more violent fights and nearby gang activity at locations like Chatfield, we believed that we needed to start a business. The business is basically to kill people who anger our clients. Hence, the "Trench Coat Mafia Hit-Men for Hire" business was created. Several weapons, such as a sawed-off pump-action riot-gun, an AB-10 machine pistol, home made rocket launchers, swords, and daggers were gathered to help our business. Now on school grounds we can't be armed. Everyone knows that if someone is caught with a weapon they are suspended or expelled, which would not help my business at all. Therefore, using our resourceful home computers, we acquire the full name, telephone number, and address of our target. Then we hunt the target down and relocate him/her to one of several secluded areas, like the bottom of a lake.

Fund Raising

As far as costs are concerned, we can be pretty lenient. For underclassmen, the cost is $50 a day for general protection. For upperclassmen it is $20 a day. Now if you wanted someone so intimidated that they would not even get out of bed in the morning, that costs about $100. Assaults and beatings can range from $200 to $500, depending on the severity. For relocation of problem targets, the price is usually between $1,000 and $10,000. It basically depends on the location and time of the hit, as well as if there will be witnesses or if it requires us to take out a whole group of targets.

We raised enough money to start our business strongly. Most of the money came from personal reserves. We also got money from relocated targets. Weaponry we already had, and ammunition isn't too expensive these days. Political contributions are the main expense.

Advertising Campaign

Our advertising campaign is quite simple. We don't want to start a war, at least not yet, so we can only help certain groups of people. We will help whoever is willing to pay the most for our protection. It is a first-come-first-served basis. My business will reach the intended audience by word of mouth alone. That may seem like we wouldn't get many clients, but we have already made $20,000 since we started the business only a few weeks ago.

So if you need our help, just come up to me, or one of my associates, and tell us a little about yourself and your problem. We'll see what we can arrange for you.

Conclusion

The fact is that people need protection from the dangers of every-day encounters and the "Trench Coat Mafia" is willing to protect you. For a small cost, you can walk the halls knowing that you have your very own personal guards keeping a close eye on you. No one, no matter what size, will give you any trouble.

The dream started out in my car. Dylan and me were trying to drive up a very steep hill to get to some event at the top. The road up was barely wide enough for 2 lanes of traffic and there were lots of other people that I recognized mostly from my bowling class trying to get up the hill also. The road was dirty, and the sides of the road sloped upward, so there wasn't much room at all. After lots of honking, yelling, aggressive driving and racing we made it to the top of the hill and parked my car. The next event I remember was struggling to get a bowling ball from an old rack sitting near the wall of a large, open room. If you have ever seen a movie called Demon Knight, it was like the main room in the hotel in that movie. After getting a ball, we ran up an open staircase. All the while people that I don't like in school were taunting us and I had a sense that things were starting to get very tense. At the top of the stairs we no longer had the bowling ball for some reason, and we looked over the railing and fights and brawls were starting downstairs. We ran over to the corner of the ledge and lots of gunfire broke out. We heard several people being shot and a lot of evil growling and yelling. We telepathically seemed to understand that we should stay where we were and wait for a SWAT team to arrive and help us out. A few times we peaked over the ledge and bullets shredded the railing and walls around us. The downstairs was empty, but had several shadows that seemed to have evil, demented inhabitants. After a long time of waiting a team of SWAT guys came in to the ledge from a door beside us and hurried us out of the building. Somehow we were on the ground level as we ran to a few cars and vans parked outside. We looked back and the SWAT team was being shot apart by gunfire. We knew that we had to rescue ourselves since the actual rescue-team was being destroyed. We hoped into a bulky white car and sped off down the hill, just as some sort of rocket flew out of the door of the building and nuked the SWAT van. Somehow I recalled some old sheriff guy in a bronco saying something about how he would escape the mountain roads by cutting across the switchbacks, no matter how steep they were. Next thing I knew we were in this bronco truck and we did a 180 on the dirt road and started to free fall down a few levels of the mountain. We landed on a road and sped off to a quiet little mountain town a few minutes down this road. After this my memory gets a little foggy, but I remember Dylan and I standing behind a large, senile mountain man who was buying a ton of groceries at a lodge. He left a sack of liquor and a pistol on the counter as he left, and I walked up and said something like to bad he forgot these, and paid for my things and left with all of the stuff. After that I can't remember much. And I am sure there were events in between some of those that I forgot as well.

Eric Harris
Period 4
2/5/99

The battered marine sat against the wall of the personnel carrier as we drove back to the base. We had picked him up from the battle scene an hour ago, and my first thought was of how tired he must be. Every bump the carrier went over he jumped awake at full attention, ready for anything. Apparently he did not get much sleep during the days of fighting. I noticed his armor as he took it off earlier, it had scratches and holes in it. Blackened burn marks speckled the chest plate and a long greenish cut ran along the back plates. His shin guards had horizontal cuts embedded into them and one of his shoulder pads was torn in half. Amazingly his body only suffered minor wounds. It was amazing that he was still alive on account that his helmet was chipped and dented in several different places. His body was almost mumbling, "Thank God or Kevlar" as he sat sleeping. His clothes were shredded and the steel toes in his boots were almost falling out. His strong arms had bandages all over them and his gloves had been worn through across the knuckles and the lower thumb. He had mumbled something about "around ten-thousand rounds" as the dim-witted lieutenant asked him how many rounds he had fired during an attempted de-briefing. His shotgun lay beside him, and his pulse rifle on the other side, both were still warm from repeated usage earlier. His standard-issue pistol was holstered, but apparently he had used and lost all five of his clips. There were a few splashes of dried blood on his body, most of it was not his own though. Signs of quite a few close-encounters that turned ugly. I noticed something odd when we tugged him aboard. His left pocket made a jingling sound whenever he moved, which I later realized was filled with dog-tags that he collected from his fallen platoon. As he pulled them out to give to the lieutenant, I saw that one was ripped in half, and another had a rather large hole in the center of it. After emptying his pockets he started describing some of his

165

Eric Harris
Period 4
2/23/99

The forest green field was hot under the sun.

The game was in its 2nd overtime.

Five soccer balls were already destroyed from heavy pounding.

Injured players were being treated on the sideline.

Orders that were being yelled by coaches and players confused us.

Time was running low, as was our resources.

The ball must go through the enemy lines.

Overhead we saw aircraft flying by.

All going in our direction, seeming to give us more power.

Their defenses were so strong.

None of our attacks could punch through.

We tried several different kinds of tactics.

Through pure luck, as always, we made it through.

The defenses were smashed and we punched through to the goal.

As we celebrated our victory, we felt sorry for the other team.

But that was just too bad for them.

Other Writings

Ich bin Gott!! hey bro whats going on. Florida huh.
Send me a postcard or something. your a bastard
for leavin us but hey, if you have a chance to get
out of this shithole, take it. learn some Deutsch, but
never disrespect it, or ic will blow up DOOM rules
I hate everything unless I say otherwise. hey dont follow
your dreams or goals or injof that shit, follow your fucking
animal instincts. if it moves kill it, if it doesn't, burn it.
kein mitleid !!! God damn not an angel when I die

RAMMS+IEN   BUCK DICH

"wake me up in Anarchy"   "Fire!!!" hey, if
you get a good comp down there, lets Dm in Doom,
I bet your dad would pray for it!! God I fucking
hate people   kick some, take some, and get some

REB

— Kristi ➤ Baby —

Guten fuckin tag. Frau sucks. but German rules!
thanks for letting me copy allIIIII that stuff in Deutsch, Hist and Chem.
Kritzer sure is one Helluva spaz huh. well, our junior year is at an end,
woop-de-flippin-do-da. we will be top of the food chain soon. hey,
stay away from those Frostys (██████), they might explode some day by
no fault of mine! and you could get hurt. hey, your smart, do something cool
when you grow up. Gott weiss ich will kein Engel sein. oh well. ready for
some philosophy? not yet? ok... ████████ and ████ need to burn, those pricks will
get whats coming soon. thanks for listening to my problems and shit, bla bla—other
nice thoughts—yadda wadda so so so... ok, time for philosophy: Nihilism, Anarchism,
and several others are all wrapped up into 1 ball called my head. society wants
to get rid of any human instincts we may have. like Kritzer said a few times, the
industrial age and factories and shit, all to better the community and lessen the
human part of life. "sit in order, be respectful, don't talk outloud, drive safely,
don't run, don't lie, bla bla don't don't" why the FUCK not!! we are humans, we
should use our brains for something besides memorizing cube roots. the things
that put us above animals is our brains, and society wants to flatten it out. they
dont want thinkers and dreamers, only thinkers and dreamers who think and
dream about how to be successful and be a good citizen. anyone who shows
more thoughts or emotion than the norm is said to be weird or crazy, wrong! they
are just more in touch w/ their humanity. and people who think they can sum
up mankind in simple lame quotes piss me off. like "there are 2 kinds of people...
the quick and the dead... the smart and the dumb,... leaders and followers..."
well you fucks are wrong!! the only 2 kinds of people are male and Female!!!!!
the rest is B.S. follow your instincts, be free from all, listen to no one, be
SELF AWARE!! step back and look at what you are doing, do you look
stupid? smart? silly? foolish? thats why I acted like I did at After prom. have
you ever watched, actually watched someone dance? it is ridiculo...lus.
people are funny, they want to be accepted. don't be afraid to judge people.
either. people say you shouldn't judge others because thats not how they are
on the inside... well oh fucking well and to flippin bad, your impression of someone
is what they seem like, and if they are to caught up and stupid to have their
true self most obvious, then thats their choice. if they look like a lame gothic
black devil wannabe then damnit thats what they want you to think and
booom, verdict mine. well, how was that for a trip through the mind of a wise one?
I hope you liked it, if you didn't I dont care anyway!! Ha Ha Ha Ha Ha Ha Ha Ha

J. + die   sehen du später   ⅁ ⅃ ⅂

Dear Mr. Ricky Becker,

Hello, my name is Eric Harris. On a Friday night in late-January my friend and I broke into your utility van and stole several items while it was parked at Deer Creek Canyon Road and Wadsworth. I am writing this letter partly because I have been ordered to from my diversion officer, but mostly because I strongly feel I owe you an apology and explanation.

I believe that you felt a great deal of anger and disappointment when you learned of our act. Anger because someone you did not know was in your car and rummaging through your personal belongings. Disappointment because you thought your car would have been safe at the parking lot where it was and it wasn't. If it was my car that was broken into, I would have felt extreme anger, frustration, and a sense of invasion. I would have felt uneasy driving in my car again knowing that someone else was in it without my permission. I am truly sorry for that.

The reason why I chose to do such a stupid thing is that I did not think. I did not realize the consequences of such a crime, and I let the stupid side of me take over. Maybe I thought I wouldn't be caught, or that I could get away. I realized very soon afterwards what I had done and how utterly stupid it was. At home, my parents and everyone else that knew me was shocked that I did something like that. My parents lost almost all their trust in me and I was grounded for two months. Besides that I have lost many of my privileges and freedom that I enjoyed before this happened. I am now enrolled in the diversion program for one full year. I have 45 hours of community service to complete and several courses and classes to attend over the course of my enrollment.

Once again I would like to say that I am truly sorry for what I have done and for any inconvenience I have caused you, your family, or your company.

Respectfully,

Eric Harris

Eric O. Harris ████████████████ ███████

    Me and Dylan Klebold were at a church off of Kendall and
Ken Caryl with Zach Heckler listening to music. We then left the
church (Me and Dylan) and proceeded to the North west corner of Wadsworth
and Deer Creek Canyon Road. We parked in the gravel and stayed there (in my
car) for a few minutes listening to a new music CD. We noticed a
white van to the West and a red truck to the East of our position. We got out
of my car and looked around for something to do. We found some beer bottles and
we broke those for about 15 minutes. We then went back up to my car and
Dylan suggested that we should steal some of the objects in the white van.
At first I was very uncomfortable and questioning with the thought. I became
more interested within about 3 minutes and we then decided to break the passenger
window with our fists. I looked for cars and I saw a white car come from
the west and pull up beside the red truck. Dylan and I waited in our car for
the white car to leave, after about 5 minutes a person got out of the car
and into the red truck, then both the truck and the car left going westbound.
We then got out of my car and I went out into the street and looked for
cars as Dylan hit the window with his left fist 3 times. Then I came over and
tried to hit it, one time. Then we decided to get a rock to use. We went North
about 20 feet and Dylan found a rock big enough to have to hold in 2 hands.
I went back to look for cars as Dylan broke the window on his 6th try.
I then stood by my driver door and looked for cars while Dylan reached
through the window and took items from the car and placed them in
my back seat. After about 15 minutes (aprox) Dylan opened the door twice
to get 2 more items and put them in my car. We then left the area and
went to the open space area and parked up there. We then began to review
the items and I suggested we put them into my trunk. That is when the officer
confronted us.
    (the items)

Eric Harris

175

The anger management class I took was helpful in many ways. I feel the instructors were well qualified for this class and the class size was not too big. I learned several things about how drugs and alcohol contribute to violence, and how to avoid using drugs and alcohol. I felt like the class was focused more on people who had committed violent crimes and people who use drugs and alcohol, rather than being more broad. Nevertheless I still learned what anger is, how to recognize it, and how to deal with it. Violence is expensive, along with anger. Committing violent crimes brings forth fees, bills, and punishment that have very deep affects on that person, not to mention the emotional turmoil it causes. I learned the four stages of anger; tension building, verbal escalation, physical escalation, and opportunity for change. I believe the most valuable part of this class was thinking up ideas for ways to control anger and for ways to release stress in a non-violent manner. Things such as writing, taking a walk, talking, lifting weights, listening to different music, and exercising are all good ways to vent anger. We also discussed the positive and negative results of anger and violence. Another thing we discussed was "triggers." Triggers are defined as warnings or symptoms that one experiences when getting angry. Things like quick breathing, tunnel vision, muscles tighten, and teeth clench. I feel that all of the suggestions can all be helpful, but the main part of anger management comes from the individual. If the person does not want to control his/her anger, then it can be a problem. The person must want to control his/her anger and actually want to not be violent or angry. It all starts in the person's mind. I have learned that thousands of suggestions are worthless if you still believe in violence. I am happy to say that with the help in this class, and several other diversion-related experiences, I do want to try to control my anger.

	i will get over him
REB DoMiNe:	ok
	good question
	i am not sure
	prolly just when he compliments me
	but i get so aggrivated with him sometimes
	i dont think that i am in love really
REB DoMiNe:	alright.
REB DoMiNe:	doesnt sound like it
	no it doesnt
REB DoMiNe:	but then again, remember this:
REB DoMiNe:	love in my view means something different to everyone. what one person calls true love can
REB DoMiNe:	be just another cheap thrill to another
	i think i am just obsessed with the idea of a great boyfriend and hes the closest i got
	yeah i guess your right
REB DoMiNe:	hm, that might be it
REB DoMiNe:	might just want love so much we exagerate our feelings
REB DoMiNe:	and romantisize them
	i think that i am just comfortable with him and right now i dont feel comforatable about
	much
REB DoMiNe:	why do you feel comfortable with him?
REB DoMiNe:	in othre words..what is so great about Mr. ████?
	cus i know he likes me as a person
	we can talk about anything
	life goals
	hes alot like you
	only there
REB DoMiNe:	damn
	and hes fun
REB DoMiNe:	mhmm
	we can goof off or have a deep conversation
	see i am really insecure
REB DoMiNe:	it doesnt seem like he can have a deep conv.
	and so when he tells me that i am his best friend and stuff it makes me feel needed
REB DoMiNe:	just seems that he would say things like "yeah...i agree....yeah...uh huh....yeah"
REB DoMiNe:	yeah.
REB DoMiNe:	well, i can see that
	it is easier to have a deep conversation with people that i met in person in person because i need to look into their eyes
REB DoMiNe:	ah.
	i need to see what they are feeling
	i dont know
	he has such beautiful eyes
REB DoMiNe:	you see, i have never had any conv.s like this in real life
	i fall into them when i look at him
REB DoMiNe:	so i wouldnt know.
	really never
REB DoMiNe:	nope.
	do you not have many close girl friends
REB DoMiNe:	just conversations at school about school things
	wow
REB DoMiNe:	no, i hardly have any

177

that seems strange to me
i think with things like this it is easier to talk to people of the opposite sex
i am not sure though
REB DoMiNe: heh. i have a bigass feeling you would hate quiet a few people here
alot of fake people
REB DoMiNe: mhm.
that dont think
REB DoMiNe: followers, airheads, losers, dumbasses
REB DoMiNe: yep
REB DoMiNe: they only think about social life instead of life life
ahh that is so annoying
REB DoMiNe: mmmhm
i hate people like that
i am so glad that you arnt like that
REB DoMiNe: as am i
it would be scary cus i prolly never would have met you
REB DoMiNe: call it fate or call it a coincidence...but i call it damn cool
REB DoMiNe: and good
no kidding
REB DoMiNe: so, what do you think when you look at the stars?
REB DoMiNe: (to start a new topic)
i tink wow they are so pretty
REB DoMiNe: ...i hope thats not all...
i have no idea about another species
REB DoMiNe: go on
i dont see how there couldnt be the universe is so big
REB DoMiNe: mhm
but then i wonder why havnt we found em yet
REB DoMiNe: ah
ya know i mean we have been searching for so long
REB DoMiNe: yeah
REB DoMiNe: and if there is other life, why havent they tried to contact us?
i know why havnt they tried to find us
REB DoMiNe: u think because they dont want to?
how do they live, communitcate, think, act look like?
i am not sure really
mbe they already found us adn didnt like us
REB DoMiNe: could be
REB DoMiNe: i know thats what i would think
yeah i would think man as a whole this planet sucks and the people are pretty
damn stupid
REB DoMiNe: yyyyyyyyep
we only use 10% of our brain, that i jst dont get
REB DoMiNe: yeah.
REB DoMiNe: and the people that use more than 10% are called crazy
REB DoMiNe: or stupid even!
i know
or freak
REB DoMiNe: mhm
REB DoMiNe: its all backasswards
lol
that is a funny word
i will have to use it sometime

REB DoMiNe: you and me are the ones who should be running the world, not all these lameass lying politic

REB DoMiNe: heh

yah that would be so cool wed have all the answers

REB DoMiNe: i would love to be the ultimate judge...and say if a person lives or dies

REB DoMiNe: be godlike

yeah could i be your goddess

REB DoMiNe: "you'll be godlike"-KMFDM

REB DoMiNe: hell yeah

ho yeah

REB DoMiNe: like my quotes in my profile say, its only cool if i say so and it only sucks if i say so

i would love to hold someones life in my hand

REB DoMiNe: me too.

hey hold on i want to read your prof

REB DoMiNe: and say "you dont deserve to live, you are worthless, die"

do you know how many people i would do that to

the world would be a much smaller place

REB DoMiNe: someone once told me no one is worthless, maybe so, but they are definitely pointless

REB DoMiNe: there would be about 100 people left on earth if we could do that.

REB DoMiNe: have you ever seen that movie made for tv "the Stand" by steven king?

no

i dont think that people are worthless but i agree pointless

REB DoMiNe: check it out sometime. it has a nice view of the world after 98% of it is dead

like their life is going nowhere

REB DoMiNe: yeah. and they only are helpful because of their "job"

but some of them dont even have jobs

REB DoMiNe: like, yeah thanks you made a movie, so the flip what

and half of them could be replaced by robots

REB DoMiNe: yes, very true

███████████ hey so whats up

REB DoMiNe: wow im so glad i found u online. here i was just about to mail this to you:

REB DoMiNe: Well, i wrote my mom a 2 page note last night and put it on the counter. i told her about our conversations and why i stay up so late and how its my life and i am in control of it and a lot of other stuff that they have been bitching at me about. so we will have to see what they say

REB DoMiNe: about that when they get home from work tonight. im happy, i finally got the courage to tell my parents what i really think. i put it on paper so they wouldnt think i was "talking back" or haveing a "bad attitude" or something.

███████████ wow i am so proud of you

REB DoMiNe: thanks!

███████████ well you have to tell me evrything they say

REB DoMiNe: ok i will

███████████ so you have to tell me bout your dream world

REB DoMiNe: alright. how long can you be online right now, i mean do we have time to talk?

███████████ yeah i got all day no plans

REB DoMiNe: awesome. ok picture this: (typing)

REB DoMiNe: your in a large rectangular room, about 10 feet by 4 feet. it reminds you of the inside of a hull of a boat. there are old computer screens around you on the walls. except something is different about them, they are futuristic looking, but yet hundreds of years old. they are covered with dust and mold and vines. the only light in the room is from a full moonthat seems to dance around in the sky, so the shadows are all creeping around you. now, in the front of the room, and on the ground, are

REB DoMiNe: windows, you can see out the windows and you are looking onto a vast sea. large hill of water going uuup and doowwwn constantly, the only sound is the wind and the movement of the water. the room that you are in is moving, like a blimp would. and you are just standing there, staring out into the sea.

REB DoMiNe: that is one place i have imagined i would like to be.

███████████ wow kind of gloomy

REB DoMiNe: yeah. but its still nice. no people at all. kind of like, everyone is dead and has been for centuries.

███████████ wow that does sound nice

REB DoMiNe: .....can only wish.

███████████ i would love that but i would need some people

REB DoMiNe: eventually i would only want 1 or 2 people.

███████████ i think i would want 4or5

REB DoMiNe: it would be tough to decide who though.

███████████ not so much for me

███████████ i keep my friends close

REB DoMiNe: what kind of people would you want with you?

███████████ i know for sure my best friends

███████████ and you

REB DoMiNe: =] thanks.

███████████ sure

███████████ i hope you could stand my friends

REB DoMiNe: if everyone was dead except say 4 or 5 of us. would you want to build up a new human race or eventually let us go extinct?

███████████ i think i would want us to go extinct but it would be inevitable that people would have sex

REB DoMiNe: true.

REB DoMiNe: maybe if we were all sterile. (couldnt reproduce)

███████████ it just is inevitable

███████████ he he

REB DoMiNe: yeah.

███████████ smoking seeds makes you sterile

███████████ and i think all stupids should be steril anywy

REB DoMiNe: yeah, in our dreams. it would be great if we were that lucky

REB DoMiNe: i dont think i would want to bring a child into this world.

███████████ he he been around hte world and found that only stupid people are breeding

▮▮▮▮	why too many stupids
REB DoMiNe:	maybe its natures way.
REB DoMiNe:	yeah.
REB DoMiNe:	jst the world itself.
REB DoMiNe:	i dont know.
REB DoMiNe:	but i think i would want us to go extinct also.
▮▮▮▮	i know what you mean we are all peices of shit
REB DoMiNe:	but i would definitely leave behind some things.
▮▮▮▮	yeah
REB DoMiNe:	like ancient civilizations have done. (pyramids, stone hedge, etc)
REB DoMiNe:	rrrrrrr. i just wish i could actually DO this instead of just DREAM about it all
▮▮▮▮	yeah i always wonder what we have done and left behind that others will wonder about
REB DoMiNe:	lately we havent left anything worth leaving.
▮▮▮▮	i know
REB DoMiNe:	just buildings. yey doggie.
▮▮▮▮	yey doggie?
REB DoMiNe:	woopdy doo. woo fucking hoo. big deal etc etc
▮▮▮▮	oh ok
▮▮▮▮	i am a little slow at times
REB DoMiNe:	why cant we make anything like the pyramids any more.
REB DoMiNe:	oh dont worry, i can be slow as hell sometimes.
▮▮▮▮	he he
▮▮▮▮	i thin we are just incapable of making anything amazing
REB DoMiNe:	i think yer right.
REB DoMiNe:	we only make things that "look" neat. nothing has any depth or meaning.
▮▮▮▮	yep just as long as it is good on the surface
REB DoMiNe:	mhm
▮▮▮▮	but all that shimmers is not gold
REB DoMiNe:	yeah....silver too. heh.
REB DoMiNe:	atleast in societies mind
▮▮▮▮	yeo
▮▮▮▮	yep
REB DoMiNe:	.........ugh
▮▮▮▮	what that mean
REB DoMiNe:	nothin really. just thinking.
REB DoMiNe:	bout what we were talkin about
▮▮▮▮	makes me mad too

181

OH my gosh, I forgot to call you huh?

REB DoMiNe: yup.

I am so so sorry...let me explain...

REB DoMiNe: oh ok.

both ██████ and one of my other friends came in tonight to ask me to go out and I told both of them no way because i wanted to go home and take a shower and just relax and I was thinking the whole shift that I was gonna call you and I just forgot after those two left around 8..I am sooo sorry :-(

REB DoMiNe: aah. doooont worry. i understand.

I feel so bad though, please don't be mad

my mom is going to braid my hair real quick....I'll be back in like five

REB DoMiNe: oh dont worry. we gota do something though...you owwwwe me nowwww=]

REB DoMiNe: ok. i should still be on

Ok I'm back

REB DoMiNe: ok cool.

REB DoMiNe: so were you very busy tonight at work?

yeah it was, but there were four of us

REB DoMiNe: so.....

REB DoMiNe: how is life treating you today?

pretty good, kinda sad because I started packing up my room

REB DoMiNe: aah. getting ready to leave huh.

yep, I have about three weeks to pack it all up though, I am leaving for most of August until right when I have to go up to CSU

REB DoMiNe: so wait, where are you going in august then?

to Wisconsin, I used to live there, I am going to stay with all of my relatives for two weeks to visit

REB DoMiNe: aah. thats great.

so what did you do today?

REB DoMiNe: ah not much. made a few calls and finally got my paycheck from tortilla wraps.

yeah I saw that sheet in the drawer, what was all of that about

REB DoMiNe: helped my mom pack too, she leaves for steamboat springs tomorrow morning

REB DoMiNe: well when ████████ired me, he never gave me the W-2 form to fill out, so i had to fill that out like around the beginning of this month and i couldnt get it to him until like monday...

REB DoMiNe: uh oh ████████ just got on.

yeah I know, I had to work with him for a half an hour today

REB DoMiNe: harrrr har. =]

he was being lazy like usual and me and ████████ oth had to re-do what he attempted when he left

REB DoMiNe: that sucks

I'm used to it with him, are you two friends at all?

REB DoMiNe: wellll. kind of yeah and kind of no.

REB DoMiNe: we have never even done anything together so not really.

REB DoMiNe: and from how i see he treats others...no not really.

that is what I though!

thought!

REB DoMiNe: =]

REB DoMiNe: what you doin tomorrow?

I am going to Idaho Springs with my family to meet some old friends from Kansas who are staying in the mountains. We are going to Beau Jo's pizza

I have to go to tattered cover in the morningq

REB DoMiNe: so uhhh, pretty un-eventful day huh. kind of boring i see...heh.

yep, pretty boring!

REB DoMiNe: heheh

what are you up to tomorrow

REB DoMiNe: i got a diversion meeting, i need to get my new medication, i work at blackjack, and my dad gets back from oklahoma tomorrow night so i need to drop my car off at SW plaza.

sorry about that, someone just called me

REB DoMiNe: you're just to popular.=]
              oh please
REB DoMiNe: so are you lookin forward to CSU?
              I am really really excited, especially to get out of this house
REB DoMiNe: yeah
REB DoMiNe: lucky. i got another year still.
              hahaha! you going to college?
REB DoMiNe: mmm. not sure yet. probly not. maybe just a 2 year college or something small. major in
computers graphics or something. but im almost positive not a 4year deal.
              I know your dream is to work at Tortilla Wraps for the rest of your life!
REB DoMiNe: oh yeah man...SSSShhhh dont tell though!!
              it will be our little secret!
REB DoMiNe: thanks! hehheh
REB DoMiNe: so what got you interested in.....communications was it?
              yeah and journalism,broadcast journalism or magazine journalism or advertising
REB DoMiNe: wow. you sure know what your doin huh. well that is very cool. good luck.
              well I hope I still like it when I get to college :-)
REB DoMiNe: yeah. i hear people change majors a lot once they are in college....not to get ya all nervous or
anything..
              that has already made me nervous, thanks though!
REB DoMiNe: heh.
              what do you REALLY want to do then
REB DoMiNe: well what i REALLY want to do is go on a nice long vacation with someone for a few months.
maybe costa rica or something. even a nice long road trip. but i just want to leave denver and all the damn people
for a while. kind of take a break ya know?
              I suggest you do that then
REB DoMiNe: buuut. i guess something to do with computers. maybe games, maybe graphics, maybe internet.
kind of wide area.
REB DoMiNe: mm. thanks.
              do you do any of that stuff now?
REB DoMiNe: yeah. i am pretty familiar with computers right now.
REB DoMiNe: especially computer games..heheh.
              you make games?
REB DoMiNe: oh no. but i play a few games in particular a lot.
              which games?
REB DoMiNe: mostly doom2. but i play quake and quake2 and duke nukem also.
REB DoMiNe: ever heard of them?
              nope, don't play computer games really
REB DoMiNe: yeah. gee your wierd, all the other girls i know are always on the computer!!! heheh. justkidin
              sorry!
REB DoMiNe: gawd jen.
              what?
REB DoMiNe: heh. nothing.
REB DoMiNe: but yeah. im usually doing something with doom2. but i love making graphics and stuff too.
              what kind of graphics?
REB DoMiNe: umm. hm. kind of hard to explain. i like very intense, deep, colorful, graphics. things that are out
of a dream or something from deep space.
REB DoMiNe: things that make you go "awwhhhhhhhhhhh...... ..thats. ..aaaawwwesome"
              that sounds pretty cool
REB DoMiNe: arrg, hey, have you ever had a dream that you just cant stop thinking about? i had this wierd
daydream today and i cant stop thinking about it.
              what was the dream?
REB DoMiNe: you really want to hear it?
              yeah

REB DoMiNe: alright. cool. gimme a sec to type it all out.
                       ok
REB DoMiNe: ok, i am walking through this very deep forest at night time...i am wearing all this military gear
like im a marine or something...there are these big flares going off way up high in the air and they are flying
through the sky so there are shadows dancing all around. then i come out onto this beach that reminds me of one of
those marine life posters with all the dolphins, whales, stars, oceans and everything. i look up into the stars and they
are everywhere, like
REB DoMiNe: 10 times as many stars as you have ever seen. then i hear this voice saying "watch out for the
flares and have a swell time!" and i get launched into space right into the stars.
                       that is pretty crazy, I don't usually remember that much detail in my dreams, just bits and pieces
REB DoMiNe: same here. i cant belive i remembered all that. sounds kind of fun though..i guess
                       that is a fun dream...I just get flashbacks during the day if I dream and that is all I think about
them
REB DoMiNe: yeah.
REB DoMiNe: hey, can i ask you a kind of personal, "deeper" question?
                       sure
REB DoMiNe: · what do you think about when you look at the sky at night, when theres no clouds out and you can
see all the stars?
                       I'm not sure if I should answer that
REB DoMiNe: ? what do you mean...
REB DoMiNe: im sorry if i said something wrong...forget i ever asked it.
                       it's just that my mom keeps walking in here and I feel kinda weird when she sits next to me to talk
it I am typing stuff like that
REB DoMiNe: oh. yeah i know how you feel. my mom does that too.
                       my dad is out of town and I think she is lonely
REB DoMiNe: so i didnt like....offend or scare or anger you did i?
REB DoMiNe: thats so sad
                       no, not at all
REB DoMiNe: phew. heh. sorry to put you in a kind of wierd position. you dont have to answer that if you dont
want to.
                       no worries
REB DoMiNe: coo
REB DoMiNe: hey, tell yer mom i said "hi" if shes still there!
                       she is in the room right next to me, I told her

=: did i make your hit list yet?
nope, yer on my "semper Fi" list. but ████████ still is in
the top 5, along with this **asshole named** /███ or ███ or something.
semper Fidelis ? always-Faithful. ~~into~~ of the ~~District~~ 's fine, he knows

who is this guy? →   that. he wants off, or
just some faggot punk ska skater   rather, he doesn't want
shitface who always makes fun of my   to die anytime soon
kind so I told him to shut the fuck   He will always be under the gun and in
up about it, and he is such a disrespectful   the sights since he hit me in the face,
smart ass and today he comes up and says   even though it didn't hurt at all. until I got
"whats up" in his little smart ass tone so   to hit him back I will always be pissed at
I yelled at him   him. and his dick head friend too; if they
          want "off" then tell them to show some fuckin
          respect to their elders (me and dylan) and never
          make another smart ass remark about us or to us.

if your going to be pissed @ me for being w/ ███, then that is your
thing, but i think that it's stupid. i'm still the same person i didn't
change just b/c i'm w/ him, but you are going to do what you will.
exactly. but I didn't think you would go out w/ someone like
him. but oh fuckin well es ist mir scheiss egal. does he still want
me to be nice to him? i'm sorry i let you down, but i'm happy
w/ ... for now, he never wanted you to be nice to him, he
just didn't want you to kill him (he's definately scared of you)
well if he will let me punch him in the face and _not_ tell a single
authoritive figure (not get me in trouble) then I will be happy. I'll
even fuckin say "Hi" to him when he's w/ you. he'll get down to
around "#90" on my "shit list" which is basically neutral. his friend
is another story though. i'll tell him, but i don't know ███ is a dick & i don't
give a shit about him, so you can do what you will. to him
oh we will. I don't expect ████████ to let me do that either,
so until he does not a damn thing will change.

your religion? - jean. that's cool, i'd probably the same way if i was
me   I just dont want the little fuck going to admin. or the
cops and start whining that we are threatning him or intimidating him.
because if i get in ANY more trouble w/ cops I will fuckin ~~lose~~ lose it.

Hi. I have a few things I really want to say but I never seem to be able to say them in person.

Even though I have only known you for a few weeks, and have hardly had any time to really *know* you, I would really like to get to know you much better. Actually when we worked together Monday night I wanted to ask you to just hang out for a while after work and maybe just talk. Like about that guy that you mentioned, the one that you met on AOL, or about work, school, people, anything. I just really wanted to spend some time with you. But, since your friend stopped by I assumed that you and her would be leaving together so I just left without saying anything. You see, I just hope that you feel the same. I am just kind of going on a hunch here, but I hope I'm right. I don't know if you like talking…or just to me… or what. From what I gather from people at work and by just being there, I see that almost every guy there flirts constantly with you or at least tries. And I try too, just to make you smile, but I have never been good at "flirting" or even just talking. I see that you are a very busy girl, and have a great family and nice friends, and you seem to like to talk about what your thinking, but so far, have been cut off short. You see, I have never understood why girls spend more time with guys who just look good and flirt a lot then with guys who actually have something intelligent to say and are a little "deeper" than most other guys. Oh well. I guess what I am trying to say is… if you have time in your life to just sit down, relax, and talk with a guy who cares a lot about you, and if you want to, let me know. Because I really want to get to know you, and who knows, maybe even "go out." If you don't…. just don't say anything. I'll understand, I'm used to it. Well, bye for now, maybe ill see you at work sometime this week. Please reply, or call, if you want to do something.

-Love Eric.

ID Software,

      Hello, my name is REB. I have been playing your mega-hit Doom for about four and a half years now, and no matter what new games are invented and sold, I always have come back to doom2. The atmosphere and over-all feel of the game is still unmatched in my books. I have been creating my own levels and patches for about three years, and am still going strong. I have read all four books published by ID software about the Doom story. Fly and Arlene, and their adventures. I have noticed now that Quake is the new "story" in the ID books. However, I have been wondering for the past four years if a Doom 3 has even been considered by ID Software. Just imagine, all the old baddies and guns from doom, all the old textures and environments that made doom have such an impact, all of them on today's and tomorrow's newest gaming engines. Imps, humans, demons, spiders, all of them remade into an engine like the one used for quake 2. If it's a story line that kept you from making Doom 3, that is the least of your problems in my opinion. If the Doom novels aren't enough, or suitable, then I am positive there are hundreds of legitimate stories out there. Even I could come up with enough of a plot to make another Doom game. The plutonium pack and such were great, but they were still all on the same doom engine. I believe that the world of the space marine should be taken one step higher, or one lift higher. How many times have you wanted to look up and down, go underwater, see the "other" side of the doom eye, climb on top of the E1M8 star, and so many other things in doom? Maybe it is just a fantasy of mine, but then again, it is so very possible to make it real. If you need workers for doom levels or for graphics, I could even be a start. With my background and love for the game, I don't think there are many people at all in the world who know more about Doom than I do. I may not be able to make Quake 2 levels, but my doom levels could be one hell of an inspiration for new worlds. So, in conclusion, I have 3 questions...

1: Has it ever been considered that a Doom 3 could be made on an engine like or better than Quake's?

2: Is it possible to make even a Doom add-on for Quake, Quake 2, or other games of the kind?

3: How about a Doom movie?

Please reply as soon as possible, and if it is at all possible, try to have the creators of the original Doom and Doom 2 read this letter.

P.S. Would you like some screen shots of my latest doom levels, "Tier?" Maybe ID could use some of these levels...

                ---Loyal Doomer, REB.

```
                                    |
                                    |
                                    |
                                    |
                                    |
                          ----------|----------
                                    |
                                    |
                                    |
                                    |
```

==

Title   : TIER
Filename   : TIER.WAD
Author   : REB
Email Address   : REBdomine@aol.com
Misc. Author Info : I have been playing doom since November of 1994, so it is
                    basically my life. These levels are better than anything you have
                    ever seen before. I don't want to brag about my own sh*t, but
                    these levels come from the Herrgott of DOOM himself...so just
                    play each one, and dont miss any rooms, and you'll see why I say
                    these are the best levels ever.
How to Play   : Load up the dehacked patch and run "doom2 -file tier.wad -fast
                  -warp 01" and if you are using DM.exe to do a deathmatch or coop
                  game, run "dm.exe -fast". Anything else, you figure it out on
                  yer own.
Description   : Tier is a 7 level patch for doom2. It has 6 new monsteres, 2 new
                  guns, 9 new gory sprites, a few new sounds, new music, and tons of
                  new textures. The theme for these levels is totally Phobos-base
                  post-war UAC lab type stuff. So just imagine returning to good
                  old episode 1 of doom with a ton of new twists. I even put in an
                  actual part of the orginal doom in the first level. It's very
                  nice, and not to hard to find. Lots of the rooms and secrets in
                  this place come directly from my imagination, so you are basically
                  running around in my own world. I live in this place. I mean a
                  person could write a freakin book on all of the symbolism and
                  double-meanings used in these levels. So show some respect, ya
                  bastages.

                  Advice from REB:

                  First things first, use the f*ckin map. You will never find
                  all of the secrets or atleast above 80% without it. Almost
                  all of the secrets are visible on the map, and they aren't
                  to hard to find.
                  Second: Each level has 4 symbols in it, locate all of them
                  and you are Godlike.
                  Third: Watch the demo.
                  Forth: If you are playing with fast mode on, and you should be,
                  you can NOT save your game, if you do save it some wierd ass bug
                  f*cks up the game and some tweeky stuff happens to it, so don't
                  save when on fast.
                  Fifth: Remember this about the machine gunners: They have bad
                  aim when you are more than about 5-10 feet away. So use that
                  to your advantage. Plus watch the first demo to find out how to
                  beat the blue key battlefield in map3.
                  Sixth: Do not try to use the cheat codes, except for idclev.
                  They have all been changed besides that one, so if you try to
                  type one in the game will bomb you out. If you are having a hard
                  time beating a level, then play it without fast mode on, so then
                  you can save your game and it'll be easier. I want you people to

see everything in every level, not get your asses kicked every
other room.

Story   : Once the demon was destroyed on Earth the war seemed over for
you. However, the re-taking of Earth had just begun. Helping
out here and there with teams of marines to take over our lost
cities, you grew tired of the same old battles. When you heard
reports that Phobos was becoming an active base for demons again,
you made a final decision. You will return to Phobos and finish
the job. You will destroy every damn monster on the whole
friggin rock and take over every base that you missed during the
first siege. What do you have to live for anyway? Every friend
you had was wasted on Phobos and your family was killed on Earth,
so why the hell not? 7 installations were skipped during your
first battle. You knew that a few teams made it over to those
bases, but all of them were killed off before you even made it
through the hanger. So you pack up a few things and head on back
to Phobos. The 9 bases that were already passed through are
basically in the same condition you left them in, which was only
a few weeks ago. The new bases that you are going to have been
"worked on" a little by the aliens. So expect some unusual
architecture and probably some ambushes. They know you're
coming. One other thing, keep an eye out for new weaponry.
There are 2 UAC weapons that you saw training videos on months
ago, but never found in the bases. One is an earlier version
of the BFG9000, and the other is a modified plasma rifle. Both,
as you remember, are very good at getting rid of enemies real
damn quick.

Additional Credits to   : VoDkA, DevilMan, Grunt, ID Software, the creators of EdMap, BSP,
Wintex, PSP 5, DeHacked, and DCK. KMFDM, RAMMS+EIN, NIN, Orbital,
The Orb, The Future Sound Of London, Steven Spielberg, Slim Jims,
Salsa Sunflower Seeds, Coke, and the authors of the DooM novels.

===

* Play Information *

Map Number   : MAP01-MAP07, game ends after map7 is completed!
Single Player   : Yes
Cooperative 2-4 Player : Yes
Deathmatch 2-4 Player   : Yes
Difficulty Settings   : Yes, don't wuss out.
New Sounds   : Yes
New Graphics   : Yes
New Music   : Yes
New Weapons   : Yes, the gun of God and the RFG
New Monsters   : Yes, a red machine gunner, an unstable Former Human,
                            a hyperactive Lost Soul, a new breed of Imps to play with the
                            old ones, a sentry, and the spidermind had a few adjustments.
Demos Replaced   : All

* Construction *

Base   : New levels from scratch
Editor(s) used : EdMap, BSP, Wintex, Dehacked, and DCK to fix a few f*ckin bugs.
Known Bugs   : The only thing I know of is that the game gets screwed up when it
                    is saved while on fast mode. Other than that, it should be fine.

As I walked through the broken door entrance to the final military installation, I realized that this hellish experience was almost over. The invasion was stopped, all of the aliens were dead, and whatever wasn't dead was waiting for me ahead. While I was leaning against a granite wall in a large calmly lit room, I scanned over the dozens of marine bodies that scattered the floor in front of me. A last, futile, stand that wasn't enough to ward off the alien attacks. Bullet shells sprinkled the floor, on top of the carpet of blood. I must go on, to fight whatever waited ahead, I am the only one left on humanity's side of the battle. The bright room ahead suggested that I wouldn't have anywhere to hide once I showed myself. I almost laid down beside my fallen comrades and just went to sleep, as some of them appeared to be. But that would mean that they bad guys would win, and I just could not allow that to happen. So I gathered up all the bullets and superior firepower I could scavenge off of the dead soldiers, or what was left of them, and prepared myself for the last battle.

As I entered the last military base on the moon, I came upon a hellish sight. Bodies of my former marine buddies were scattered across the stone floor. The deathly dark glow of light from above provided barely enough light to notice the blood and flesh splattered on the large slabs of granite that passed for walls. The platoon had tried to barricade themselves in, but with the alien fire coming through two gigantic windows and with a blitzkrieg of monsters in the small doorway between the windows, the marines couldn't hold them. Arms, legs, and heads were tossed about as if a small child turned on a blender with no lid in the middle of the room. Some were burnt off, some torn, some eaten. Even though the mass of alien bodies outside the room was at least 10 times the marines', they still fell. I must be crazy to fight this war; I must be out of my battered mind. How could one soldier stop all of these monsters? There must be someway out of here that doesn't involve firepower. It is just too much, all the death and destruction. It's pointless, there's no way, no way at all. I can't fight anymore-let them take Earth-I'll stay here on my little moon-along with my squad of dead soldiers.

<HTML><FONT SIZE=5 PTSIZE=14>--send this to everyone you know. the more who know about me the better. </FONT><FONT SIZE=3 PTSIZE=10>1. Full name: Eric Harris 2. Nicknames: REB, reverend, indigo, WAR 3. Birthplace: wichita, KS 4. Birthday: 4/9/81 5. Where Do You Live Now?: hell. a few days ago people called it littleton.(denver) 6. Parent(s): Wayne and Kathy 7. Sibling(s): Kevin 8. Looks: 5'10" 140. skinny but handsom, some say 9. Favorite Animal(s): Dogs, bald eagles. 10. Favorite TV Show(s): i hate TV 11. Favorite Kind(s) Of Music: industrial 12. Favorite Movie(s): Lots highway 13. School: former Columbine high school. 14. Future School: none 15. Future Job: none 16. Boyfriend/Girlfriend: Nope 17. Best Buds: the 4 horsemen. me(war), vodka(death), ████(famine), ████(pestilence) 18. Favorite Candy: slim jims. 19. Hobbies: doom. guns. 20. Things You Collect: fireworks. gun powder. 21. Do You Have A Personal Phone Line: kinda. its the computer line too. 22. Favorite Body Part Of The Opposite Sex.? legs. 23. Any Tattoos And Where Of What?: Not yet. 24. Piercing(s) And Where?: hell no. 25. What Do You Sleep in?: Boxers 26. Do you like Chain Letters: burn em. 27. Best Advice: follow instincts. 28. Favorite Quotes: kill em all. lets rock. BUCK DICH 29. Non-Sport Activity You Enjoy: Computer, shooting. 30. Dream Car: hummer. 31. Favorite Thing To Do In Spring: shoot stuff. blow up stuff. 32. What's Your Bedtime: whenever 33. Where Do You Shop?: try not to. army surplus or hot topics. even though its a trendy little place. 34. Coke or Pepsi: Coke 35. Favorite Thing(s) To Wear?: black stuff and sunglasses. 36. Favorite Subject(s) In School?: Bowling. 37. Favorite Color(s): black 38. Favorite People To Talk To Online ████ n CSU 39. Root-Beer or Dr. Pepper? toss em both. 40. Do You Shave? when i feel like it. 41. Favorite Vacation Spot(s): mountains. 42. Favorite Family Member(s): Bro 43. Did You Eat Paint Chips When Y ou Were a Kid? No 44. Favorite CD you own: a custom burn of gothic industrial stuff 45. The ONE Person Who You Hate The Most: are cops one person? 46. Favorite Food(s): salsa sunflower seeds and slim jims. 47. Who Is The Hottest Guy or Girl In The World? ████ something. a few others. 48. What Is Your Favorite Salad Dressing?: ranch 49. When You Die, Do You Wanna Be Buried or Burned Into Ashes? Burned 50. Do You Believe In Aliens?: you bet your probbed ass i do 51. If You Had The Chance To Professionally Do Something, What would You Do?: blow up things. 52. Things You Obsess Over: guns bombs doom. 53. Favorite Day of the Week: friday 54. A Teacher You Hate: ████ 55. Favorite Disney Movie: burn em all 56. What Is Your Favorite Season?: summer 57. What Toppings Do You Like On Your Pizza?: peproni and green peps. 58. Do You Like Your School Food Itself (As In The District Food): 59. If You Could Live Anywhere, Where Would You Live? phobos 60. Favorite Thing(s) To Do On Weekends: bowl and get stoned 61. Favorite Thing(s) To Get Clean up: eh? 62. Favorite Magazine(s): guns and ammo, penthouse, time. 63. Favorite Flower(s): this chinese one i saw. 64. Favorite Number(s): 7, 666 65. Favorite Ice Cream flavor(s): cookie dough!!!! 66. What Kind of Guys/Girls Are You Attracted to?: sexy and fun ones. 68. What's Your Most Embarrassing Moment? getting arrested 69. If You Could Change One Thing About Yourself What Would It be? weight. 70. Do You Eat Breakfast First Then Brush Your Teeth or Brush first ten eat breakfast: i eat breakfast and then i brush my teeth 71. Favorite Time of Day: 2am. 72. Can A Guy and Girl Be Just "Best Friends?": i guess. 73. Do You Ask the Girl / Guy Out Or Do You Wait For Them To Come To You?: ask em out. 74. Do You Mind Paying For Sex? depends on who its with, but no not really. 75. What's The Most Important thing In Someone's Personality?: compassion 76. Do you have a pager or cell phone? hell no 77. Favorite Sport: soccer 78. What Was the Best Gift You Ever Received? my 86 honda prelude 79. How Long Did This Letter Take You To Finish?: 5 min 80. What Did You Listen To While Completing It?: Nothing 81. Are you or would you like to be married in the near future (next 5 years)? no 82. Don't u just hate how psychics never win the lottery? would rather rob.</FONT><FONT SIZE=5 PTSIZE=14></HTML>AOLF

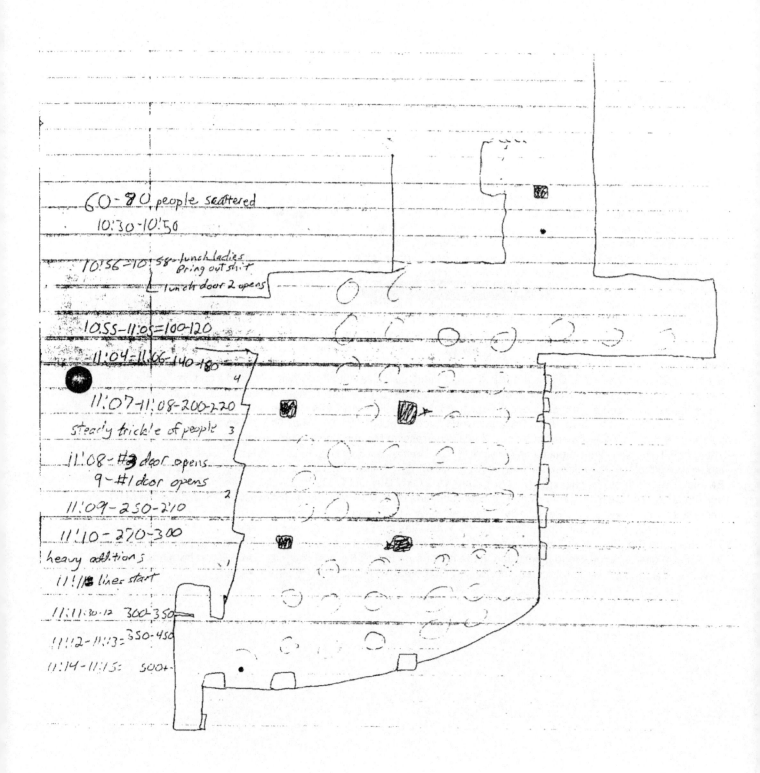

60-80 people scattered
10:30-10:50

10:56-10:58 → lunch ladies
bring out shit
↳ lunch door 2 opens

10:55-11:05 = 100-120

11:04-11:06-140-180

11:07-11:08-200-220
steady trickle of people   3

11:08-#3 door opens
9-#1 door opens

11:09-250-270

11:10-270-300
heavy additions
11:11 lines start

11:11:30-12 300-350

11:12-11:13= 350-450

11:14-11:15: 500+

Part II: Dylan Klebold

Journal

Fact: People are so unaware .... well, Ignorance is
bliss I guess.... that would explain my depression
~Dylan

About in the middle

A Virtual Book
EXISTENCES
By: Dylan

Properties: This Book cannot be
opened by anyone Not
Dylan. Some supernatural
force blocks common people
from entering

<<~VaDiket~>>
<<~DyLaN~>>

196

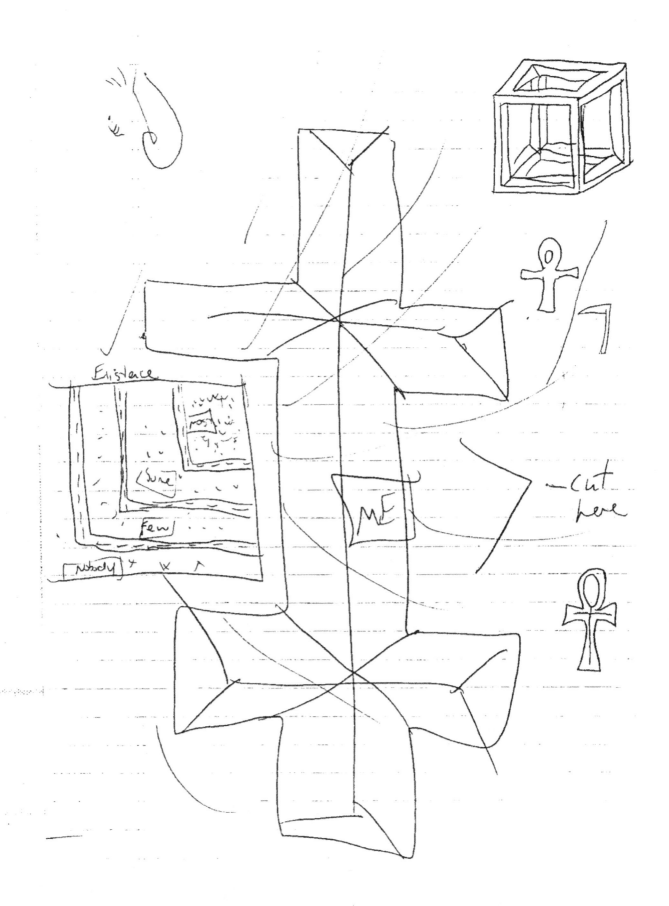

Existence

Sure

Few

Nobody

ME

— cut here

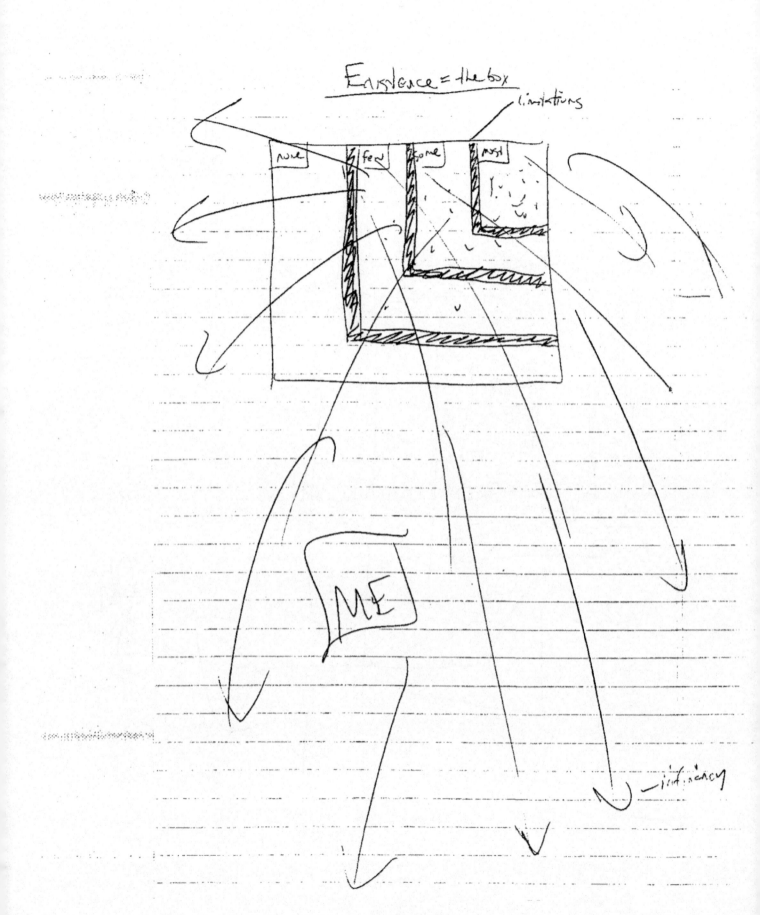

EC THOUGHTZOS

Ah yes, this is me writing... just writing, nobody technically did anything, just i felt like throwing out my thoughts — this is a weird time, weird life, weird existence. As I sit here (partially drunk on a screwdriver) i think a bit. Think... Think... that's all my life is, just shitloads of thinking... all the time... my mind never stops... music runs 24/7 (apt a sleep), just songs i hear not necessarily good or bad, & thinking... about the asshole ███████ in Gym class, how he worries me, about driving & my family, about friends & doings with them, about girls i know (mainly ████ & ████) how i know i can never have them, yet i can still dream... I do shit to supposedly 'cleanse' myself in a spiritual, moral sort of way (deleting the 'unacceptable' on my comp, not getting drunk for periods of time, trying not to ridicule/make fun of people ███████ at school, yet it does nothing to help my life — mostly. My existence is shit to me... now how i feel that i am in eternal suffering, in infinite directions in infinite realities — yet these realities are like artificial, induced by thought. how everything connects, yet it's all so far apart... & i sit & think... Science is the way to find solutions to everything, right? I still think that, yet i see different views of shit now — like the mind — yet if the mind is viewed scientifically... Now I dwell in the past... thinking of good & bad memories

thought
picture

⟳→

a lot on the past things— i've always had a
thing for the past — how it reacts to the present &
the future — or rather vice versa. I wonder how/when
i got so fucked up in my mind, existence, problem —
when Dylan Benet Klebold got covered up by this
~~entity~~ containing Dylan's body... as i see the people
at school — some good, some bad — i see how different
i am (aren't we all you'll say) yet i'm on such
a greater scale of difference than everyone else (as you all
know, i'd guess)

entity

just rather shallow existences compared to mine (maybe)
like ignorance = bliss — they don't know beyond this world
(how i do in my mind — is in reality, or in this existence)
yet we each are lacking something that the other possesses —
i lack the true human nature that Dylan owned, & they
lack the our-developed mind/imagination/knowledge too!
I don't fit in here — thinking of suicide gives me
hope, that i'll be in my place wherever i go after
this life — that i'll finally not be at war w. myself,
the world, the universe — my mind, body, everywhere, everything
at PEACE in me — my soul (existence). & the picture
is ~~still~~ monotonous, go to school, be scared & nervous (spelled wrong)
hoping that people ~~can~~ can accept me... that i can
accept them... the NIN song Piggy is good on
thought writing... The Lost Highway sounds like a
voice about me.... i'm gonna write letters bye — cc - LUDRAC

Dr. Thought 2 : Fear

Well well, back at it, yes (you say) ~~the~~ whoever
the fuck "you" is, but yea. My life is still
fucked, in case you care... maybe,... (not?) I have
just lost fuckin 45$ & Before that I lost my zippo
& knife - (i did get those back) why the fuck is he
being such an ASSHOLE??? (god i guess whoever
is the being which controls shit) life's fucking me over
big time & it pisses me off. Oooh god i HATE
my life, i want to die really bad right now - lets see
what i have that's good : A nice family, a good house,
food, a couple good friends, & possessions, whats bad -
no girls (friends or girlfriends), no other friends except a few,
nobody accepting me even though i wish to be accepted,
me doing badly & being intimidated in any & all sports,
me looking weird & acting shy — BIG problem,

thought
picture

me getting bad grades, having no ambition
of life, thats the big shit. Anyway...

I was Mr. Cutter tonight — I have 11
depressions on my right hand now, & my fav.
contrasting symbol ~~because~~ because it is so true & means
so much — The battle between good & bad never
ends... OK enough bitchin ~~to~~ well im not ~~the~~ done
yet. ok so ... I dont KNOW what i do wrong with
people (mainly women) — its like they are set out to
hate & ignore me, i never know what to say or do.

▮ is soo fuckin lucky he has no idea how I suffer...

ok heres some poetry..... this is a display
of one man in search of answers, never finding them,
yet in hoplelessness understands things .....

Existence..... what a strange word. He, set
out by determination & curiosity, knows no existence,
knows nothing relevent to himself. The petty declarations
of others & everything on this world, in this world, he knows
the answers to. Yet they have no purpose to him. He seeks
knowledge of the unthinkable, of the unbelievable, of the
unknown. He explores the everything... using his mind, the
most powerful tool known to him. Not a physical barrier blocking
the limits of exploration, time then thought then dimensions ....
the everything is his realm. Yet, the more he thinks, hoping
to find answers to his questions, the more come up. Amazingly,
the petty things mean much to him at this time, how he
wants to be normal, not this transciever of the everything.
Then occuring to him, the answer. How everything is connected
yet seperate. By experiencing the petty others' actions,
reactions, emotions, doings, ~~thoughts~~ and thoughts, he sets
a mental picture of what, in his mind, is a cycle.
◎ Existence is a great hall, life is one of the ~~rooms~~, death
is passing thru the doors, & the ever-existant compulsion of
everything is the curiosity to keep moving down the hall thru
the doors, exploring rooms, down this never-ending hall. Questions
make answers, answers conceive questions and at long last he is content
TTYL <<-VODKA->>

Thoughts

Yo.... whassup.... Idunnohere... Know whats
weird? Everyone knows everyone — I swear —
like im an outkast, & everyone is conspiring against
me.... Check it... (this isnt good, but i need to write
so here.....

Within the known limits of time...
within the conceived boundaries of space....
the average human thinks those are the settings
of existence... Yet the ponderer, the outkast, the
believer, helps out the human. "Think not of
2 dimensions" says the ponderer, "but of 3, as your
world is conceived of 3 dimensions, so is mine. While
you explore the immediate physical boundaries of your
body, you see in your 3 dimensions — L, W, & H. Yet I,
who is more mentally open to anything, see my 3
dimensions — my realm of thought — Time, Space, & THOUGHT.
Thought is the most powerful thing that exists — anything
conceivable can be produced, anything & everything is
possible, even in your physical world." After this so
called "lecture", the common man feels confused, empty,
& unaware. Yet those are the best emotions of a ponderer.
The real difference is, a true ponderer will explore these emotions &
bother in a dream.   what caused
                                              them.

Miles & miles of neverending grass, like a
wheat. A warm sunshine, a happy feeling in the presence,
Absolutely nothing wrong, nothing ever is contrary 180°
to normal life. No awareness, just pure bliss,
unexplainable bliss, The only challenges are no challenge,
& then ..... BAM!... realization sets in, the world is the greatest
                                              punishment. Life

[Hypnosis place — ~~It~~ is a sky — with one large cloud, & sort of a cloud made chair — the sun is at the head of the chair — 10 o'clock into the sky — Below, i sometimes see myself & the green (forest green) earth — sorta a city, yet I hear nothing. I relax on this chair — actually like a chaise — & i am talking — to what? I don't know — it's just there, i have the feeling that i know them, even though I consciously don't — & we talk like we are the same person — He has my soul....

thought box

The everlasting contrast....

Dark. Light. God. Lucifer. Heaven. Hell. GOOD. BAD. Yes, the everlasting contrast. Since existance has known, the fight between good & evil has continued. Obviously this fight can never end. Good things turn bad, bad things become good, the "people" on the earth see it as a battle they can win. HA fuckin' morons. If people looked at history they would see what happens. I think too much, I understand, I am GOD compared to some of these unpredictable brainless zombies. Yet, the actions of them interest me, like a kid w. a new toy. Another contrast, more of a ~~pro~~ paradox, actually, like the advanced go for the undeveloped's realm, while some of the morons become everything dwellers — but exceptions to every rule & this IS a BIG exception — most morons never change — they never decide to live in the "everything" frame of mind!

Carter   <<—vodka—

<<-VoDkA->> 's Thoughts

[The ████████ situation]

It is not good for me right now (like it
ever is) ... but anyway .... My best friend
ever: the friend who shared, experimented, laughed,
took chances with & appreciated me more than
any friend ever did has been ordained ...."passed
on" ... in my back. Ever since ████ (who i wouldn't
mind killing) has loved him.... that's the only place
hes been: with her... If anyone had any idea
how sad I am..... I mean: we were the TEAM
when him & I first were friends, well I
finally found someone who was like me:
who appreciated me & shared very common
interests. Ever since 7th grade, i've felt
lonely... when ████ came around, I finally
felt happiness (sometimes)...we did cigars, drinking,
sabotage to houses, EVERYTHING for the
first time together & now that he's "passed on"
i feel so lonely, w/o a friend. Oh well, maybe
he'll come around ————> ...I hope.

[Boob]

————> for this topic

That's All....maybe i'll
reverse this again ....————>

Ô = ████████ = ὸ
<<- VoDkA ->>

My 1st love ??

OH My God...... I am almost sure
I am in love w ███████████ Hehehe...
such a strange name, like mine... Yes, everything
about her I love. From her good body to her
§ Almost? perfect face, her charm, her wit
& swimming, her NOT Being popular, Her friends
(who I know) some — B just hope she likes
me as much as I ❤ LOVE Her, I think
of her every second of every day, I want
to be with her, I imagine me & her doing
things together, the sound of her laugh, I
picture her face, I love her. If
soulmates exist, then I think I've found
mine. I hope she likes Techno... ☺)

███████, I love you
~Dylan

my thoughts

oooh god i want to die sooo bad... such a sad, desolate, lonely
unsalvageable i feel i am... not fair, NOT FAIR!!!
I never got just one day of happiness!! I never got it...

let's sum up my life... the most miserable existence in the history
of time.... my best friend has ditched me forever, lost in bettering
himself & having/enjoying/taking for granted his love.... Ive NEVER
been this... not too times near this... they look at me
like im a stranger,.... I helped them both out thru life, & they
left me in the abyss of suffering when i gave them the boot out.
The one who I thought was my true love, ████████ is not.
Such a sell of what i want the most... The meanst trick was
played on me - a fake love... She in reality doesn't give a
good f%ck about me... doesn't even know me..... I have no
happiness, no ambitions, no friends, & no LOVE !!! ████
can get me that som I hope, i wanna use it on a poor
SOB. I know... his name is vodka, dylan is his name too.
what else can I do/give... i stopped the pornography I
try not to pick on people, Obviously atleast one power is
against me. ████████... funny how Ive been
thinking about her one the last few days... giving myself
false realities that she, or her MIGHT have liked me just a
bit... my sadu I have always been hated, by everyone &
everything, just never aware..... Goodbye all the crushes ive
ever had, just shells... images, no truths... BUT

WHY ? Yes you can read
this, why did you show

A dark time,
infinite sadness,
I want to find
love.

Ignorance is bliss
happiness is ambition
desolation is knowledge
pain is acceptance
despair is anger
denial is helpless
martyrism is hope for others
advantages^(taken) are causes of martyrism
revenge is sorrow
death is a reprieve
life is a punishment
other's ~~own~~ achievements are tormentations
people are alike
i am different.   —Dylan

me is a god, a god of sadness
exiled to this eternal hell
the people i helped, abandon me
i am denied what i want,
to love & to be happy
being made a human
without the possibility of BEING human
the cruellest of all punishments
to some, i am crazy
it is so clear, yet so foggy
everything's connected, separated
I am the only interpreter of this
I'd rather have nothing than be nothing
some say godliness isn't nothing
humanity is the same thing i long for
I just want something i can never have
The story of my existence.   —Dylan

208

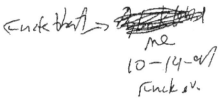

Thoughts

Me, sorry I didn't write, A SHITLOAD in my existence since.
Ok.. hell & back ... ive been to the zombie bliss side .... &
I hate it as much if not more than the numeress part.
I'm back now... a taste of what I thought i want...
wrong. Possible girlfriends are coming then ██████..
i'll give the story shit up in a second. i want TRUE
one...I just want something i can never have ... true true
I hate everything, why cant i die... not rain. I want
pure bliss... to be cuddling w. ██████ who i think i love
deeper than ever... I was hollow, thought i was right. another
form of the Downward Spiral - deeper & deeper it goes.
to cuddle w. her - to be one w. her, to love, just laying
there. I need a jm. This is a mixed entry... I
should feel happy, but shit brought me
down. I feel terrible. The Lost Highway
apparently repeats itself. I want dirk.
now. ██████ lucky bastard gets a
perfect soulmate, who he can admit
FUCKIN SUICIDE to. & I got rejected for being
honest about fuckin love for jake. From the wrong people
maybe... ██████ & ██████ Anyway...heres a
2 poems.

FUCK
me Die
me

Awareness signs the warrant for suffering. Why is it that the zombies achieve something we wants (overdeveloped me). They can love, why can't i? The true existor lives in solitude, always aware, always infinite, always looking for his love. Peace might be the ultimate destination. destination unknown... i want happiness. Abandonment is present for the martyr, my thoughts i~~loss~~ i~~live~~want to ~~live~~ in. I want to find a room in the great hall & stay there w. my love forever. sadness seems infinite, & the shell of happiness shines around. Yet the true despair overcomes in this lifetime. How tragic for me.

RelCKln DumASS shallhead

presto shit it not workin

golden pee so dead

ylons shit cool water

srtall

Reek

FUCK

No emotions. not caring.
yet another stage in this
shit like suicide~ pfunk 6t

This

Farther & farther distant— Thats whats happenin... me & everything that zombies consider real... just images, not life. Soon i will ~~be at~~ peace i hope...

Burn → ♪♪ "with all yer life sucked up around you" ♪♪ I get more depressed with each day, ♪♪ more sad... but i cant ♪♪♪♪♪
~~stop~~ ♪ ; ♪ ♪♪♪ ♪♪♪♪♪♪♪♪♪♪~~~~

Some sad i owe... All people i ever might have loved have abandoned me, my parents piss me off & have me want me to have fuckin ambition!! How can i when i get screwed & destroyed. By everything >>!!! I have no money, no happiness, no friends,... Eric will be getting another away soon... I'll have less than nothing ... how normal. I wanted to love... i wanted to be happy and ambitious and free & nice & good & ignorant... everyone abandoned me,... i have small stupid pleasures... my so called hobbies & doings... those are all thats left for me... clinging onto the smallest cracks... many people climbing up a neverending vertical cliff... ██ ██ and a plateau to every one... they walked up me to get to it. nobody will help me... only exist w. me if it suits them. i helped, why cant they? ... ██ will get me a gun, ill go on my killing spree against anyone i want. more crazy... deeper in the spiral lost highway repeating, dwelling on the beautiful past, (██ & ██ gettin drunk) w. me, everyone moves on i always ~~~~ stayed. Abandonment. this room sux. ~~~~

211

everything is as least expected. the meak are trampled on, the assholes prevail, the ~~sadistic~~ gods are deciaving, lost in my little insane asylum w. the outhouse redneck music playing... wanna die & be free w. my love... if she even exists. She probably hates me... findya noledee or a jock who treats her like shit. I remember details... nothing worth remembering i remember. I don't know my love; could be ▮▮▮ or ▮▮▮ or ▮▮▮ or ▮▮▮ or anyone. I don't know & ("to be all knowing to be kept in the dark - is op punishment")

I have lost my emotions... like in heart & the song. N.M. People eventually find happiness i never will. Does that make me a not-human? YES the god of sadness... ▮▮▮ church was so funny the rec thing w. ~~never~~

Never shes

Half existed

everything (No, Everything (everything

Ooo... Beeeer... Man I don't know what's up lately... never do in existence. All this shit w. ████ & ████ friends... so weird & different from past... yet again, that's the way in existence. I wonder if ill ever have a love... my love_ ████ got his, i don't, won't ever get mine. Here's all the people ive loved or at least liked (or thought i loved)_ all the same meaning.

████ is the newest... the purest (for now)... seems perfect for me... I seem perfect for her. I was delusional & thought she wanted out me the last day of school. oh well... my emotions are gone so much past pain alone my senses are numbed. The beauty of being numb... Let E5

one of
my
symbols

Everything { No, everything { No, everything
                              No, everything
            { No, everything { No, everything
                              No, everything

The cliff theory... everyone
trying to get higher & stable...

Existence... to understand

well well... so much changes... (like... existence).
I understand almost everything now... so close to my love –
████████ The runes have shown it, she has shown it,
i have felt it. I know the meaning of each life: To
be loved by yer love, & to be happy w/ ones self. Only
for the gods though (me, ████████ etc.) The zombies
& their society band together & try to destroy what
is superior (&what they don't understand & are afraid
of. Soon... either ill commit suicide, or ill get w/.
████████ & it will be NBK for us. My hapiness, her
hapiness _NOTHING_ else mathers. i've been caught
in. most of my crimes – xpt drinking, smoking, & the house
vandalism, & the pipe bombs. If, by fate's choice,
████████ didnt love me, id slit my wrist & blow up atlanta
strapped to my neck. Its good, understanding.
a hard road since my realization, but il gets
easier. BUT IT DOESNT! Thats part of
existence. unpredictible. Existence is pure
hell & pure heaven at the same time. i will never
stop wondering, the best highway will never end, the music in
my head will never stop... Totra ll part of existence. The half
will never end. The love will always be there. (GoD)

B LOVE HORIV/ – ITS so great
to be

society is tightening its grip on me, & soon I & [REDACTED] will/snap. We will have our revenge on society & then be free, to exist in a timeless spaceless place of pure happiness. The purpose of ~~life~~ is to be happy & be w/ your love who is equally happy. Not much more to say. Goodbye

"Almost happiness in slavery — the real people (gods) are slaves to the majority of zombies, but we know & love being superior.

"I didn't want to be a jock... I wanted the happiness that they have — & I will have something infinitely better..."

I love
her & she loves
me

(By the way, some zombies are smarter than others.)
Some manipulate... like my parents.

I am (God) [REDACTED] is (God)
& zombies will pay for
their arrogance, hate, fear, abandonment, &
distrust

██████ Thats all i think about anymore. I know that this humanity is almost over, that we will be free. We have power to make that we are the everything of purity & halcyon, & that we deserve, need, love, and exist w/o eachother. It's hard, i think that i might not be enough, my mind sometimes sets stuck on its own things, i think about human things. All i try to do is imagine the happiness between us. that is something we cannot even conceive in this toilet earth. The everything the halcyon, the happiness is ours. There will be no notes from me. Let the humans suffer w/o my knowledge of the everything.

I am trying not to think about the happiness, somehow thinking that it will destroyed it i conceive/relish into being im a human. But i love her. we are soulmates.

(Please don't skip to the back" read the note as it was written)

You don't conscionsly know who I am, & doubtedly unconsionsly too. I, who write this love you beyond infinice. I think about you all the time, how this world would be a better place ~~too~~ If you loved me as I do you. I know what you're thinking: ("some psycho wrote me this harrassing letter)" I hoped we could have been together... you seem a bit like me. Pensive quiet an observer, not wanting what is offered here. (school, life, etc.) You almost seem lonely like me. You probably have a boyfriend though, & might not have given this note another thought. I have thought you my true love for a long time now, ~~by~~ but... well... there was hesitation. You see I can't tell if you think of anyone as I do you, & if you did who that would be. Fate put me in need of you, yet this earth blocked that with uncertainties. I will go away soon, but I just had to write this to you, the ~~~~ one I truly loved. Please, for my sake, dont

It is solely ~~my~~ my decision: nobody elses,

tell anybody about this, as it was only meant for you. Also, please dont feel any guilt about my soon-to-be "absense" of this world. Oh... the ~~~~ thoughts of ~~us~~ us... doing everything together, not neccessarily anything, just to be together would have been pure ~~heaven~~ heaven I guess it's time ~~~~ to tell you who I am. I was in a class with you 1st semester, & was blessed w/ being with you in a ~~report~~. I still ~~remember~~ your laugh. Innocent, beautiful, pure. This semester I still see you ~~rarely~~ rarely. I am ~~~~ entrance during 5th period, as we both have it off. To most people, I appear ~ well ... almost scary, but thats who I ~~am~~ appear to be as people are afraid of what th don't understand. I ~~denied~~ who I was for along time. until high school ...

Anyway, you have noticed me a few times, I catch every one of these gazes w/ an open heart. I think you know who I am by ~~now~~ now. Unfortunately... ~~you~~ even if you did like me even the slightest bit, you would ~~like~~ hate me if you ~~B~~ knew who I was, I am a criminal, I have done ~~things~~ things that almost ~~nobody~~ would even think about condoning. The ~~reason~~ that I'm writing you now is that I have been caught for the crimes I comitted, & I ~~want~~ want to go to a new existence. You know what I mean. (Suicide?) I ~~have~~ have nothing

I would enjoy life knowing that you loved me.

to live for, & I won't be able to survive in this world after this legal conviction. ~~However~~ However, if it was true that you loved me as I do you,... I would find a way to survive. Anything to be with you. 99/100 chances you prob. think I'm crazy, & want to stay as far away as possible. If that's the case, then I'm very sorry for involving an innocent person in my problems, & please don't think twice. However, If you are ~~one~~ who I hoped for in my ~~dreams~~ dreams & ~~realities~~ realities, then do me a favor: ~~leave~~ leave a piece of paper in my locker, saying anything that comes to you. Well I ~~guess~~ guess this is it~ goodbye, & I love(d) you.

combo= 19-37-c

locker #857 near the library

6·8·9?

▮▮ Hakyon

I LOVE ▮▮▮▮▮▮

I love her to infinity "

I look back on my awareness journey, see the
parts & selections of my understanding --- it's
almost done, yet it is never done. I have
▮ ▮ She is my soulmate,
my love; all the imaginative Halcyons
& pure existences I have with her (& me)
are almost happiness --- I just wish I could
call her... something blocks me from calling
her... my inner self is putting up a wall
to prevent me from calling her, like a fear
of "its" truth. PS, I will overcome
all fears, doubts, & zombie-based thoughts
(oxymoron) --- I will follow my heart,
to the Halcyon, loving her. I love you
▮▮▮▮

Forever Fall, up & down
spiral

1.5 human years... so much changed in small time, my friends (of my choice) are depleting & offsprings smile like i thought they would, I am ready to be in ▓▓▓▓ The ups & downs of fate are forever, good & bad, equal me. the lost highway, & downward spiral never end. existence is like infinity times itself. ∞∞ I have passed thru this much of the ever existence this is almost a checkpoint the zombies have set their place in my mind. for the

cliff theory, I've jumped off in

and we've floated away to the halcyon the zombies will pay for their being, for their nastiness I know everything yet I know nothing & am a true god. my infinite memories, thoughts, perceivations of purity come a lot more in. now, there is pure happiness— the purpose of our existence I hate everything, hate everything, love me & ▓▓▓▓ I understand that I can never ever be a zombie, even if i wanted to. the nature of my entity. Soon we will live in the halcyon of our minds, the one thing that made me a god. Things are so simple, now that they are infinitely complicated NANANANA

I understand
whatever life everything—
F on the good
of the everything

Existences

Existence books

~~[redacted]~~ ...ate is my only master

This is prob. my last
entry. I love my
self close second to
~~[redacted]~~ my everlasting
love. goodbye

finalmen...
stop
learning

224

CR 18 Shit

This shit again, back at writing, dying just like a fucking zombie. Lately I can't change my mind from the fucking deeds of zombies - Earth, humanity, HERE. thats possbly what I think about, i hate it. i want to be free, w/ free w/... I thought it would have been Time by now. the pain multiplies infinitely, never stops. (yet(?)) in here, STILL alone, still in pain so is she. The thing i have concluded is that ✳ will decide when we should be together. ✳ decided when our existence started, it should end the same way, with us unknowing, in limbo. I love you ▓▓▓▓▓ Always hare will. The scenarios, images, pieces of happiness still come. They always will. I love her she loves me. i know she is tired of suffering as i am, it is fine. it is time. I love her. the journey, the endless journey started it has to end. we need to be happy to exist truely. I see her in perfection, the halcyons I await, endless purity. i exist as less-than nothing w/o her. —O. my humanity —O. I don't know if i should call her, or wait for ▓▓▓ ✳ to act. Yet calling her is a cycle of humanity. Im forever sorry, infinitely, about the poems. My humanity has a foot fetish & bondage extreme liking. i try to thwart it, sometimes to no effect. Yet the masturbation has stopped. I'm sorry ▓▓▓▓▓ always. I feel the happiness here, thinking of her, for brief moments, thats how i know the everything is true.

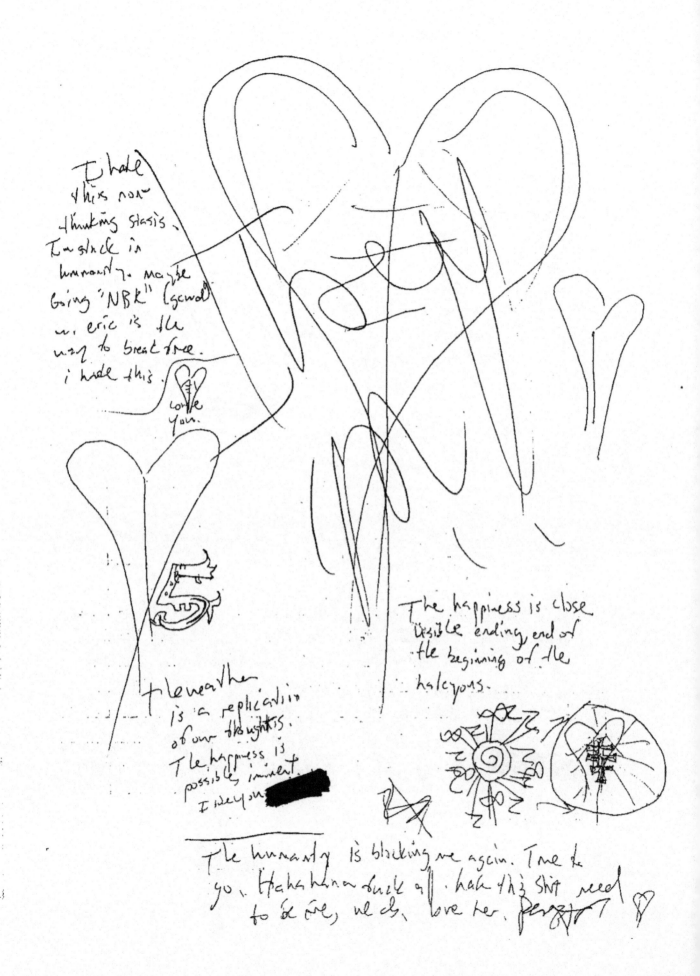

I hate
this non-
thinking stasis.
I'm stuck in
humanity. maybe
going "NBK" (scrwd
w. eric is the
way to break free.
i hate this.

love
you.

The weather
is a replication
of our thoughts.
The happiness is
possibly imment.
I love you

The happiness is close
Visible ending end of
the beginning of the
halcyons.

The humanity is blocking me again. Time to
go. Hahahaha fuck off. hate this shit need
to be one, wl us, love ya.

226

The framework of society stands above &
below me. The hardest thing to destroy, yet the
weakest thing that exists. I know that i am different,
yet i am afraid to tell the society. The possible
abandonment, persecution is not something I want to
face, yet it is so primitive to me. I guess being
yourself means letting people know about inner thoughts
too, not just opinions & fashions. (weird) I will
be free one day, in the land of purity & my happiness,
I will have a love, someone who is me in many. Someday...
Possibly thru this life, maybe another, but it will happen...

Love is more valuable than anything I know. To love is to enter a completion of oneself. I hate those who chose to destroy a love, who take it for granted. love is greater than life even. As i look for love, i feel i cant find it. ever, but something tells me i will, someday. Somewhere. As my love will find me. She feels as i do right now, i can feel it, we will be inseperable, Her & i. Whether it is ~~_____~~ or not, i think ill find it. (my love). we will be free, to explore the vast worlds of the stars. To cascade down everlong waterfalls & thru the warmest seas of pure happiness... no limits,... no limits, nothing will stop us.

228

School Work

Senior Predictions

Dylan Klebold
8-20-98
LA, per. 6
@ C.C.B, Mr. Webb

Great font — what is it?

Rea... the paper you need to use a standard font

231

Senior Predictions

As Senior year approaches for the class of 1999. As this year is just beginning, I, as well as most other seniors, am unsure as to what to expect in our last curricular school year. However, there are some things I do expect from this upcoming year. Those being having more fun for a year than previous years, college preperation, & the need for decision making about my future (career & living).

I predict that myself, as well as everyone other senior, will have more fun this school year than any others in the past. I will have more freedom, with the same basic guidelines, meaning more time for less responsibilities. (i.e. Having a later curfew, but not having to get up on weekends, like many employed adults do.) Also, the fewer hard classes on my schedule add to the non-difficulty. That, in comparison, would be 5 classes vs. 6 or 7 in previous years. Those are two of many factors that would make this year more enjoyable than years before.

Another foreshadowed aspect of my senior year would be deciding about colleges. My predicted major is in the computer field, which helps me since the demand for knowledgeable computer technicians, network administrators, & programmers is high. With that being my major, picking colleges with an acceptable technology program might prove difficult. Visiting campuses is one part of preperation. I expect to take at least two road trips around Colorado, just for looking at colleges & deciding where I would want to go. Another part of preperation would be filling out applications, & possibly taking extentions to the SATs & ACTs. I do not have any colleges in mind at this point in time, but I have not yet begun to

232

redundant

look at specific colleges yet. These & other college-oriented activities are forseen, & usually

necessary within the next year.

The crucial need for decision making within the next year is defenitely forseen. I

(probably) will be deciding what the rest of my life looks like. In these decisions are where I

would want to live. About this I have no idea yet. Another one of these decisions will be

what my career will be, & where I want to pursue that career. This partially ties in with

college preperation, unless I have an unseen change in college majors. These & other

important decisions await my response within my senior year.

(cut off
3rd page) In conclusion, senior year poses many new factors. Those being the change in my

social life, the college preperation, & the need for decision making that might tell me what my

future will look like. Although these are things that are predictable, there will

still be questions.

The Mind and Motives of Charles Manson   Dylan Klebold
                                                11-3-98
                                                L.A., Per. 6

In 1994, Oliver Stone directed a film, using a Quentin Tarantino-written script

about a pair of lover serial killers, (partially using the "Bonnie and Clyde" theme) entitled

"Natural Born Killers." This film portrayed the main two characters who, at the point

between innocent teen-ager and experienced adult, defy society, and get lost in their own

little world, killing, and robbing whoever they come across. Although still on Earth, they

live by their own morals, beliefs, and at the end of the film, expose the media and the law

for its flaws. The truth to this movie is that it was not made to reproduce the Bonnie and

Clyde theme, but it was almost an exact parallel to one man, with similar experiences in
the

late nineteen-sixties; Charles Manson. Oliver Stone stated later, in an interview related to

the movie "The idea was that he would become more like Charlie Manson." (describing an

interview with Mickey Knox, the serial killer in Natural Born Killers.) The parallels from

the film to the most stunning murders in the sixties can be seen from the similarities in the

interviews between Manson and Knox, to the setting and time period. The point being
that

the movie was later considered one of the most daring movies of all time, thus just
scraping

the surface of the severity of the story behind Charles Manson and his so-called "family."

Charles Manson was born near 1935 to an unknown father. and a prostitute. Not

much is known about his past, just abstract things. Manson went to a foster home at age

three, and his mother later was arrested for robbery. From then to the age of eighteen and past, he was moved around from foster home to foster home, juvenile prison to juvenile prison. His prison record included two counts of forgery, two counts of mail theft, check forgery, probation violation, pimping, and GTA. It was around this time in his life that he met the early members in his family.

Patricia Krenwinkle was an average girl growing up in the suburbs. She got average grades, and sang in her school's glee club. She had one sister, a mother, and their father was an insurance agent. At age eighteen, she was a secretary, and had just joined the hippie movement. She met Charles Manson at a party at the house of her sister's friend. He was playing an original, yet sad song on his guitar. She was drawn to him by his karma, mood, and attitude, which led to their sleeping together that same night. He inticed her, by words of love and happiness, to an extent that she was happy whenever he was around, and never wanted to leave him. Two days after meeting him, they, with others, left for San Francisco. 3 Transition sentence

Leslie Van Houten had a similar upbringing. She was a suburbanite, who sang in a church choir, and was later the homecoming princess at her high school. Other than the fact that her father left the family when she was young, she had an uneventful early life. At her late teenage years, she wanted more than normal girls had at that time. She heard about Manson, how he had the answers, and how closely he portrayed christ. She too met him, and fell into what might not be called "love", but possibly an obsession, with him and with the happiness that he appeared to bring with him. With Manson she later explained her actions "I followed him because I anticipated a positive change."

Others like Krenwinkle and Van Houten had gotten word of Manson's unearthly

235

beliefs and prophecies. Charles "Tex" Watson, once an All-American high school athelete, later bacame Manson's biggest believer. Lynette "Squeaky" Fromme, whose father was an Aeronautical Engineer, was also a follower, and later was the acting head of the family when Manson was not around. These people, and dozens others followed Manson out West, first to San Francisco, and then further South, winding up at a place called Spahn Ranch.

Charles Manson would later have a "family" of these followers, who literally did whatever he asked. They found happiness in his and eachother's presence. It was mainly a piece of the hippie movement, a way to stray from the norm and live opposite of what one was raised to learn. The structure was simple; he was the leader, the christ, the martyr of the group, and they listened to and did what he said. This type of control, however innocent the motives, could be considered a cult, and was later labeled as such. Yet, the main principals behind their family was, and only was, Manson's will. The Mind and Motives of Charles Manson, and society's counteractions are best described when his beliefs, his actions to support and uphold these beliefs, and society's laws to stop him are taken into account.] —T

Manson has been proclaimed by many to be insane. The question of whether or not he is insane is a question of opinion, which cannot have a "true" right answer. However, his beliefs, which fueled his and his family's actions between 1968 and 1975 conflicted with society's morals, around which this country revolves. The severity of Manson and his family's doings are reasoned behind his beliefs toward himself, his family, nature, other people, and the law.

Charles Manson, on many occasions, has compared himself to Jesus Christ. He

236

believed that he was Christ, and the world had made him suffer, just as Christ did two

thousand years ago. He also had his family believing that he was christ. He said in an

interview, when asked how he got his followers to believe that he was Jesus, "I was just

being myslf...... all men is Jesus Christ." He also believed that he was Satan, to come to

Earth and start Helter Skelter, what he called a prophetical armageddon.

His family, he believed, had two main spiritual duties: to learn to be him and to act

like him, and to also learn and believe in what he did. He and the family lived with

each other, living off, what he would consider love, for each other, and the earth. He told

them that the happiness is in love. He believed that they should, when necessary, die for

him, and not feel remorse. He preached to them that death was not bad, just another high.

The family eventually adopted these beliefs, thus putting them at his complete control.

Nature, according to Manson, was one of the most precious things in life. He

subscribed to the belief that ATWA (Air, Trees, Water, Animals) kept humans alive, and

we should treat ATWA with equal respect. He once metaphored that ATWA was a ship,

and the human wastes to the earth, pollution, and forest destruction was like a hole in the

bottom of the boat. He, when living at Spahn Ranch, would tell his family to let the

scorpions crawl over them, as they were aminals, not meant to endanger the family.

Helter Skelter, revenge were part of his beliefs. Humans had corrupted the Earth

and ATWA, and were ignorant about it. Manson had felt that society dumped him, and he

felt great rage for society, and people, and later found an anthem for his rage. When
asked

about his actions, many years after the murders, he had said that he is a part of everyone,

that he mirrors people, because they shaped him. The Beatles' "White Album" included songs (Helter Skelter, Revolution #9, Piggies, and others) that Manson felt documented his

rage toward society. When at the ranch, he and the family listened to these songs many times over. Manson thought he had heard his name being said in one of the songs. Their thoughts about Helter Skelter, or the armageddon, were brought out by these songs. In Revolution #9, he heard machine gun fire, the oinking of pigs, and a man saying "rise."

His beliefs would later incite Helter Skelter, using his family as a type of "army." Some people believe that he just brutalized people, that the murders were for no cause, and he was just insane. Yet, more than twenty-five years after he and his family were convicted, he still has the same beliefs, and still can logically explain his actions. August 9, 1969 and August 10, 1969. These two days carry a dark shadow over them. Two of the first ritual cult-style mass murders in U.S. history. The first of the two changed the mood of the entire population of L.A. for almost a year. These murders were the coming of Manson's Helter Skelter, the armageddon of the Earth.

Spahn Ranch is a small, run-down ranch near L.A. It was owned by George Spahn, who was then a decrepid, eighty-year-old wrangler, whose kids had gone away, and whose wife had died. He was depressed near death, when a group of hippies came to his door. They agreed to take care of him, and the ranch in exchange for living space. He agreed. The group, otherwise known as Manson's family, had Squeaky take the most care of George, which included cleaning, cooking, making love to him, and other various tasks. The family, which consisted of twenty-six people, began its cultish life in the desert.

"We played a lot of music, we did a lot of drugs, we loved, we were happy" replies Manson when later asked about life at the ranch. The family, did these things, and more.

They lost their humanity at the ranch. Life was lived "now". for "today." Manson told them to always "live today." The family members never talked about the past, never thought about the past or the future. The initiation of female family members was just that they joined. Male members would pick any woman they wanted and made love to them. Manson's thoughts on this was that that's what women are for, to bait the men.. The women were not allowed to deny who picked them. They had no watches, to forget time, and society. Manson would walk up to members daily, and have them mirror his actions, to try to be exactly like him. They took hundreds of acid trips. they did marajuana. and during the acid trips, he would have them reenact the crucifiction. During these times he would ask them if they would die for him, if they would "be him." The members had started to live Manson's reality. Manson would hear about the discrimination against the blacks in the South, and this was partially where he based his proof that Helter Skelter was near. the members started getting more guns, knives, and other weapons. They had lookouts at the ranch. They also robbed places to get money. Leslie Van Houten even robbed her father to get money for the cause.

By August 8, 1969, Manson had allready killed a few people for various reasons. These drug dealers, and bums that he did kill are civil compared to the two ritualistic murders, done for Helter Skelter. Manson once tried to get a record contract from a producer, living at 10050 Cielo Dr. in Bel-Air, which later failed. Manson, who had been telling the family for months that they needed to start Helter Skelter themselves. needed money to bail out a member from jail. near midnight, on August 8. he called a meeting about this. He sent Pat Krenwinkle, Susan Atkins, Linda Kasabian. and Tex Watson to

10050 Cielo Dr. to get money. He had told the women to do whatever Tex told them, and was remembered saying "I don't care how you do it, but do it, and get it done now!" Later that night, just after midnight, August 9, they pulled up to the driveway. Tex cut the telephone wires, and, bypassing the electric gate, the women scaled a fence and climbed up a hill to the yard. This house was no longer occupied by the record producer of Manson's acquaintence, but instead a beautiful new actress named Sharon Tate. Her lover and soon-to-be husband Roman Polanski, who was a movie director, was in London at the time. She was pregnant with their eight-month-old baby. She, Jay Sebring, Voytek Frykowski, and Abigail Folger were at the house for the night. Sebring was a world-wide known ~~mive~~ hair dresser, owning Sebring International. Folger was the heriess to the Folger coffee fortune. Frykowski was an actor, her lover. Back behind the house in a small shack was William Garretson, who was a caretaker of the house, who would later be an important witness. At the time when the women jumped the fence and were waiting for Tex, they heard four gunshots. He has seen Steven Parent driving up to the residence. He was an acquaintance of Garretson, coming by to visit. He was killed instantly, four shot at point-blank range. Tex then caught up with the women, and walked to the front door. It was locked, so he went through an open window next to the door, letting the women in first. They got the four people into the living room, together. Sebring, who tried to protect Sharon, was bludgeoned in the head once, then shot and stabbed by Tex. The other three people were panicked at this time. Frykowski tried to run out the back door, but was caught up to by Tex. He was clubbed in the head several times, shot, and stabbed. It was later counted that he was stabbed fifty-one times. Before his death, Abigail Folger had been tied up, and now was starting to get free. She ran out the back, pursued by Krenwinkle. She was ran down, and stabbed to death. Krenwinkle later recalled her saying "I'm allready dead..." (later found to have been stabbed twenty-eight times.) Finally, Sharon Tate, the only one left, was begging for the life of her baby to Tex, who replied "Look bitch, I have no mercy for you." He then stabbed her stabbed to death. After these five brutal murders, the killers wound up taking only seventy dollars before leaving. When returning to the ranch, Manson was remembered saying only two things; "Do you have any remorse?", and "Don't tell anyone."

"Sharon Tate, four others slain in ritualistic murders." These were the headlines the following day in the Los Angeles Times. Even the New York Times, which never printed murder cases on the cover page, printed the Tate murders on the cover for almost a week. The night of August 9, 1969, Leno Labianca and his wife, Rosemary, were driving back from a vacation at Lake Isabella. It was about 3:00 AM August 10 when they finally arrived back at their house. Manson had picked Krenwinkle, Van Houten, and Tex to go to their house. Manson still needed money, and he said that he went to a party at the neighboring house once before. He had asked Van Houten, "Can you be me, do you believe enough in me to do this?" This time, Manson came with them in a seperate car. They arrived, and walked through the front door. Tex tied up Leno, who was reading the paper in the living room. At this time, Manson had left, leaving no evidence of his presence. The two girls took Rosemary into the bedroom. Manson had told Tex "Don't scare them like last time, just kill them." Leno was stabbed to death while Rosemary was forced to listen. Tex then came in, and also stabbed her to death ~~also~~. He then handed a knife to Van Houten, who then stabbed Rosemary in the back fifteen times. Pat then went out to the dead body of Leno. She took a fork, and stabbed him on the stomach multiple times, and finally left the fork in him. No money was taken.

During the first set of murders, They had written "Piggies" and "Helter Skelter" in Tates blood on the door. In the second set, they wrote with Leno's blood "Rise". "Death to Pigs", and "Helter Skelter" on the walls before they left. These cultish writings were the only things that the police could find in common to the two murders.

By 1970, Manson and his followers had killed more people than the victims in the Tate-Labianca murders, but the severity of the two back-to-back slaughters shocked the nation. Nobody had seen killings like these. Unprovoked, uneccessary, and inhuman.

Four months after the two murderings, police finally caught up with and arrested Manson and his followers for the murders. The cultish actions and Manson's control over the family, however, didn't stop when they were all in custody of the law. It had taken years after the trials for the family to break Manson's will over them.

Manson and four of his followers were arrested four months after the murders. He, along with Tex Watson, Susan Atkins, Leslie Van Houten, and Pat Krenwinkle were charged with first degree murder counts on Steven Parent, Sharon Tate, Abigail Folger, Voytek Frykowski, Jay Sebring, Rosemary Labianca, and Leno Labianca. The main pieces of evidence were the revolver that Tex used in the Tate murders, and fingerprints around the residences. The revolver, which was later found in a field near the site, had no gun grip, which was found in three pieces at the Tate crime scene.

Along with the seven known murders, Manson and his followers had collected a "tab" of bodies around the L.A. area, for various reasons. These others include Nancy Warren, Clida Delaney, Marina Habe, Mark Walts, Gary Hinman, Donald Shea, John Haught, James Sharp, Doreen Gual, and Ronald Hughes, the lastone, in late 1970. Also, Squeaky, Manson's acting head of the family, had attempted to assassinate president Gerald Ford in 1975.

During the trial, Manson had his three female followers do many strange things to confuse the court, including carving X's in their heads, always making stupid symbols in the courtroom, and even taking full blame for all the murders. However, the prosecution, led by Vincent Bugliosi, had verbal evidence from a testimony given to them by Linda Kasabian. She, once a family member, had traded information to the prosecution for a full pardon. It was recalled that a family member screamed at her from outside the courthouse "You're going to kill us all!" After the end if the trials, Manson and his family were all found guilty, partly due to the testimony of Kasbian, and also to the evidence found. They all got the death penalty, which was abolished about a year after the trials. Their sentances

were reduced to life in prison. Since then, up until the present, Manson has been living in solitary confinement, without parole. Pat Krenwinkle, Leslie Van Houten, and Susan Atkins are still in prison, are allowed parole attempts. and never recieve them. Tex Watson

is in jail, but was allowed to marry, and has three kids.

The law of America and the state of California stopped Manson from committing

243

more murders. and mostly put an end to his family. However, the country has been shocked for twenty-five years hearing about Manson's family. The severity of the Tate-Labianca murders has never diminished, and even though the murders are credited to Manson's ideas, the innoecnt times of a hippie cult, the family's life at Spahn Ranch can also be credited to him, and his ideas.

To this day, Manson's influence over his followers, and the entire U.S. is still lingering. He always told people he was a crazy old man, but many people followed him. However, his beliefs, and the beliefs of his followers have changed in twenty years.

Cult behavior, for the most part, sprang up after Manson's family affairs in the late 1960's. One good example of the related lifestyle is David Karesh and his followers in the early 1990's. According to Krenwinkle, the scariest thing is when Manson gets a follower from the younger generation. For example, Axel Rose recorded one of Manson's songs. and wears a Manson T-shirt at concerts. "The biggest misconception is people thinking that what we did was OK." says Krenwinkle in a recent interview. double space

To this day, Manson still believes the same things he has all his life. He also says that he had no part of the Tate-Labianca murders, and that the government treated him unfairly. Manson will be in solitray confinement for the rest of his life. saying these things to countless reporters who choose to hear his side of the story.

Pat Krenwinkle, Leslie Van Houten, and Susan Atkins, the three women followers tried with Manson are all in jail to this day. They all have dropped Manson's beliefs. and live commendable lives. Atkils has converted to Christianity. Van Houten and Krenwinkle, who hold jobs, and help kids with drug problems, say "The thing about Charlie is that he says he's crazy to hide under people's awareness. In this way. he can get people to do things for him, without them questioning his motives." This is what they say happened to them, and countless others, who subscribed to Manson's beliefs. and suffered the consequences.

Manson's murder case was the most extraordinary of the time period, expecially taking into accuont the hippie era. However, the murders partially stemmed from the era. As he had so many people under his control, believeing his every word, what he thought (of) turned into a reality. Oliver Stone compliments Manson. when describing his interview with Geraldo Rivera, saying that Manson had the upper hand of the discussion the entire time. Intelligence is not one and the same with sanity. however, which might have explained Manson's retaliation against society. It is of somebody's opinion. to decide whether or not they think Manson is insane. Yet, His mind and motives can explain why he acted how he did, and why society didn't approve.

your Paper is very good allthe. little circles are Just little mistakes Just make sure you dailiorpaie

Works Cited

"Access Manson." On-Line. Available: http://www.atwa.com. 14. October 1998.

Bugliosi, Vincent. Helter Skelter. New York: W.W. Norton & Company, 1974.

"Charles Manson Page." On-line. Available: http://www.hominet/~homerb/manson.htm.
        14, October 1998.

The Manson Women. Video Cassette. A Turning Point, 199?.

Natural Born Killers: Directors Cut. Dir. Oliver Stone. With Woody Harrelson, Juilette
Lewis. Vidmark Entertainment, 1996.

The town, even at 1:00 AM, was still bustling with activity as the man dressed in black walked down the empty streets. The moon was barely visible, hiding under a shield of clouds, adding a chill to the atmosphere. What was most recognized about the man was the sound of his footsteps. Behind the conversations & noises of the town, not a sound was to be heard from him, except the dark, monotonous footsteps, combined with the jingling of his belt chains striking not only the two visible guns in their holsters, but the large bowie knife, slung in anticipation of use. The wide-brimmed hat cast a pitch-black shadow of his already dimly lit face. He wore black gloves, with a type of metal spiked-band across the knuckles. A black overcoat covered most of his body, small lines of metal & half-inch spikes layering upper portions of the shoulders, arms, and back. His boots were newly polished, and didn't look like they had been used much. He carried a black duffel bag in his right hand. He apparently had parked a car nearby, & looked ready for a small war with whoever came across his way. I have never seen anyone take this mad-max approach in the city, especially since the piggies had been called to this part of town for a series of crimes lately. Yet, in the midst of the nightlife in the center of the average-sized town, this man walked, fueled by some untold purpose, what Christians would call evil. The guns slung on his belt & belly appeared to be automatic hand guns, which were draped above rows of magazines & clips. He smoked a thin cigar, and a sweet clovesque scent eminated from his aura. He stood about six feet and four inches, and was strongly built. His face was entirely in shadow, yet even though I was unable to see his expressions, I could feel his anger, cutting thru the air like a razor. He seemed to know where he was walking, and he noticed my presence, but paid no attention, as he kept walking toward a popular bar, The Watering Hole. He stopped about 30 feet from the door, and waited. "For whom?" I wondered, as I saw them step out. He must have known their habits well, as they appeared less than a minute after he stopped walking. A group of college-preps, about nine of them, stopped in their tracks. A couple of them were mildly drunk, the rest sober. They stopped, and stared. The streetlights illuminating the bar & the sidewalk showed me a clear view of their stare, full of paralysis & fear. They knew who he was, & why he was there. The second-largest spoke up "What're you doin man..... why are you here...?" The man in black said nothing, but even at my distance, I could feel his anger growing. "You still wanted a fight huh? I meant not with weapons, I just meant a fist fight....cmon put the guns away, fuckin pussy!!" said the largest prep, his voice quavering as he spoke these works of attempted courage. Other preps could be heard muttering in the backround; "Nice trench coat dude, thats pretty cool there...."... "Dude we were jus messin around the other day chill out man... " ... "I didn't do anything, it was all them!!" ... "cmon man you wouldn't shoot us, were in the middle of a public place..." Yet, the comment I remember the most was uttered from the smallest of the group, obviously a cocky, power hungry prick. "Go ahead man! Shoot me!!! I want you to shoot me!! Heheh you wont! Goddam pussy....." It was faint at first, but grew in intensity and power as I heard the man laugh. This laugh would have made Satan cringe in Hell. For almost half a minute this laugh, spawned from the most powerful place conceiveable, filled the air, and thru the entire town, the entire world. The town activity came to a stop, and all attention was now drawn to this man. One of the preps began to slowly move back. Before I could see a reaction from the preps, the man had dropped his duffel bag, and pulled out one of the pistols with his left hand. Three shots were fired. Three shots hit the largest prep in the head. The shining of the streetlights caused a visible reflection off of the droplets of blood as they flew away from the skull. The blood splatters showered the preps buddies, as they were to paralyzed to run. The next four preps were not executed so systematically, but with more rage from the man's hand cannon than a controlled duty for a soldier. The man unloaded one of the pistols across the fronts of these four innocents, their instantly lifeless bodies dropping with remarkable speed. The shots from that gun were felt just as much as they were heard. He pulled out his other pistol, and without changing a glance, without moving his death-stare from the four other victims to go, aimed the weapon out to the side, and shot about 8 rounds. These bullets mowed down what, after he was dead, I made out to be an undercover cop with his gun slung. He then emptied the clip into two more of the preps. Then, instead of reloading & finishing the task, he set down the guns, and pulled out the knife. The blade loomed huge, even in his large grip. I now noticed that one of two still alive was the smallest of the band, who had now wet his pants, and was hyperventilating in fear. The other one tried to lunge at the man, hoping that his football tackling skills would save his life. The man sidestepped, and made two lunging slashes at him. I saw a small trickle of blood cascade out of his belly and splashing onto the concrete. His head wound was almost as bad, as the shadow formed by the bar's lighting showed blood dripping off his face. The last one, the smallest one, tried to run. The man quickly reloaded, and shot him thru the lower leg. He instantly fell, and cried in pain. The man then pulled out of the duffel bag what looked to be some type of electronic device. I saw him tweak the dials, and press a button. I heard a faint, yet powerful explosion, I would have to guess about 6 miles away. Then another one occurred closer. After recalling the night many times, I finally understood that these were diversions, to attract the cops. The last prep was bawling & trying to crawl away. The man walked up behind him. I remember the sound of the impact well. The man came down with his left hand, right on the prep's head. The metal piece did its work, as I saw his hand get buried about 2 inches into the guy's skull. The man pulled his arm out, and stood, unmoving, for about a minute. The town was utterly still, except for the faint wail of police sirens. The man picked up the bag and his clips, and proceeded to walk back the way he came. I was still, as he came my way again. He stopped, and gave me a look I will never forget. If I could face an emotion of god, it would have looked like the man. I not only saw in his face, but also felt eminating from him power, complacence, closure, and godliness. The man smiled, and in that instant, thru no endeavor of my own, I understood his actions.

quite an ending

Dylan —

I'm offended by your use of profanity. In class we had discussed the approach of using # !# !

Also, I'd like to talk to you about your story before I give you a grade. You are an excellent writer/storyteller, but I have some problems with this one.

Other Writings

Book 1°
Knee Deep in the
dead

REB!

Hooly shit... it would take me the whole fuckin book to recount & (off a) everything this year, so just the main things ill have to cover. Us & zack got the BEST fuckin spots haha fag jocks have to see their doc martins used. DIEEE This is next year's section. BLF will be fuckin chaos, video productions, — i still have the list of our videos. I cant wait to dub the new freshmen, & the holy April morning of NBK...

252

BOOK 2: HELL ON EARTH

SPECS OF LIGHT

Deimos

Fly & Arlene's shuttle

Ahhhh, my favorite book. We, the gods, will have SO much fun w. NBK!) killing enemies, blowing up stuff, killing cops !! My wrath for january's incident will be godlike. Not to mention our revenge in the commons. GAWWWD soooo many people need to die. & Now, a fun look at the past! (Science-Desk style.) ((You know what I hate??) PEOPLE!!. YEAA !!.))

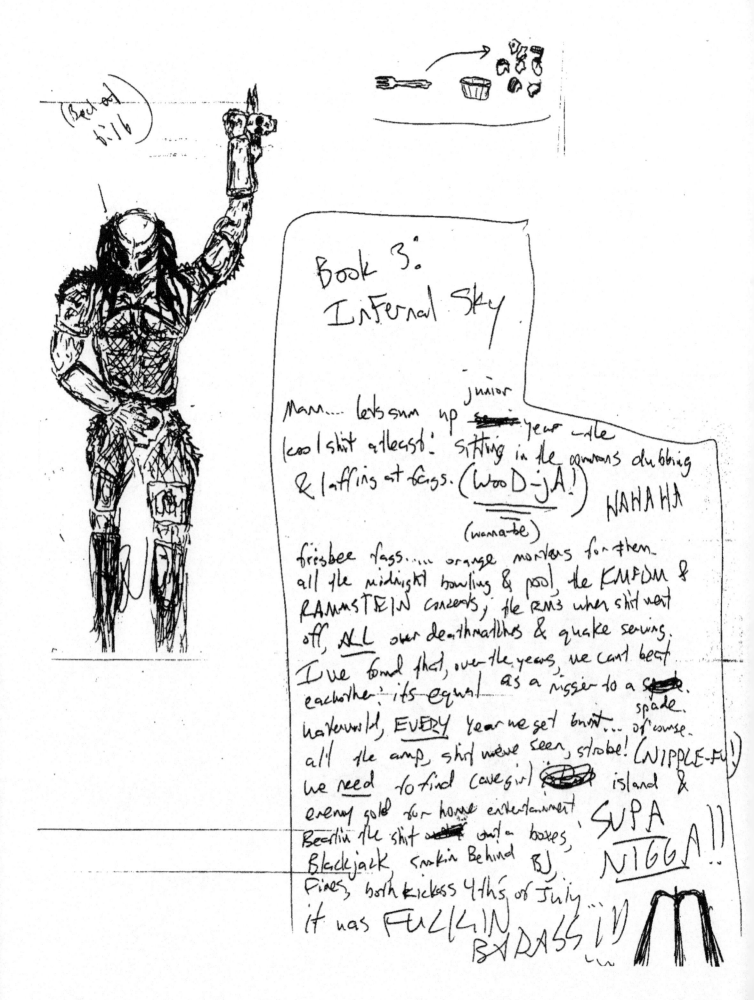

(Back of)
5:16

Book 3:
Infernal Sky

Mann.... lets sum up ~~senior~~ junior year while cool shit atleast! sitting in the commons dubbing & laffing at fags. (WooD-jA!)   HAHAHA
(wanabe)

frisbee tags.... orange monkers for them all the midnight bowling & pool, the KMFDM & RAMMSTEIN concerts; the RM3 when shit went off, ALL over deathmatches & quake serving. I've found that, over the years, we cant beat eachother; its equal as a nigger to a ~~spade~~. spade. waterworld, EVERY year we get burnt... of course. all the amp, shit weve seen, strobe! (NIPPLE-FU) we need to find cavegirl island & enemy gold for home entertainment. Beerlin the shit ~~out~~ out a boxes, Blackjack smokin Behind BJ, Fires, both kickass 4ths of July... it was FUCKIN BADASS!!! SUPA NIGGA!!

/ MY Quotes!!! →

• Dead people are the best companions, other than weapons.

• There are more than 99 ways to die.....
   & I thought of them!

• If I don't like them, then they should change, or die.

• My black blood & yer white flesh.

• I find a similarity between people & doom zombies

• Stupid people are here for my amusement.

• The reason people piss me off is to test my trigger finger, & my adrenaline.

Book 4 : Endgame (?....)

Last written book, none to come. I won't bore you w. advice shit you allready know. NBK will be the ultimate revenge, to our shitlists, the pigs, everyone! we'll fuckin 'Take care of business' to be sure. So, Indigo, As we near the day of fate .... AAAAA FUCK IT!.

just let it come. They will know when gods get pissed off... the little pussies will feel the shotguns shells & the Bullet/s. Just like that little right of comm. service. They ned to die soo bad. Now they will!

LATER.... <<—VODKA—>>

(GREEN)

256

CHIGGO'S GROOVE

I'm the GOD of mp3's!! you'll never beat me... Albertsons has funny hehehe DIE connie...

I will put efried beans in the toilet & rotten eggs!! everywhere...
dam zippo haha

sup men... surfboards, bitchez... rrr
Busy ola Mac on the beach I want the TV! hehehe set it another time
j/k I'll hehehe

Straight playin kill jiggy kill puffy kill hanson
kill RICHARD MARX!!

AAAAAA!!...

Later
<-- VODKA -->
Dylan

Just A Day

I seem to remember our fishing trips well. They were always preempted, never extemporaneously brought out by my father the night before his intended day of relaxation. How could one look forward to a trip if they did not know about it? Go to bed early, we have to get up at 5! Under normal circumstances, this would bring out a barrage of arguments & pouting, but going fishing was not an everyday thing. This was a good thing, as opposed to getting up for school or some other bulls*$t. I would wake up to black skies & coffee bean aromas making their way around the house. I never liked coffee, but I loved the smell. I would dine on fancy breakfast cuisine, otherwise known as Cocoa Puffs. My brother would already be up, trying to impress our father by forcing down the coffee he hadn't grown to like yet. I always remember my brother trying to impress everyone, and myself thinking what a waste of time that would be. I would go to the garage & get my fishing tackle together, & throw it in the back of our '74 Ram. By then my brother & father would have all the food & coolers ready, & they would be packing, ready to go. The drives up to the mountains were always peaceful, a certain halcyon hibernating within the tall peaks & the armies of pine trees. It seemed back then that when the world changed, these mountains would never move. They would remain at peace with themselves, and with anyone who would respect them. We arrived at the lake, but I don't remember what the name of it is. The lake is almost vacant, except for a few repulsive, suburbanite a$$holes. I never liked those kind of people, they always seemed to ruin the serenity of the lake. I loved the water. I never went swimming, but the water was an escape in itself. Every so often, the waves would form a small pattern, & change current in an odd shape. I would always cast into those spots, thinking that the fish were more attracted to these parts of the water. Time to bait. I never liked salmon eggs, too much gooey crap that gets on your fingers. Instead, I went with a lour, even though this was a lake. I knew I would have to use eggs if I wanted any fish, but that didn't matter at the time. Cast, Reel, etc. countless times, and my mind would wander to wherever it would want to go. Time seemed to stop when I was fishing. The lake, the mountains, the trees, all the wildlife s$*t that people seemed to take for granted, was here. Now. It was if their presence was necessary for me to be content. Time to go!. Done. Back to society. No regrets, though. Nature shared the secret serenity with someone who was actually observant enough to notice. Sucks for everyone else.

Soundwave 800 cartrige

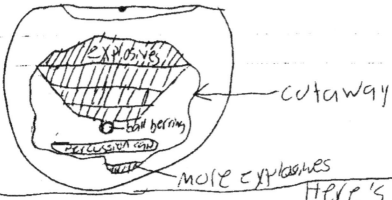

explosive
cutaway
ball berring
PERCUSSION cap
more explosives

Here's what happens

sound waves
from ball berring
hitting pecussion
cap.

YOU GOT A CAPSULE. OF SOUNDWAVES

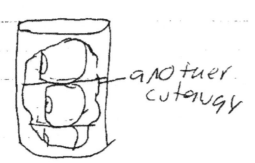

Capsule
(size of
barrel)
another
cutaway

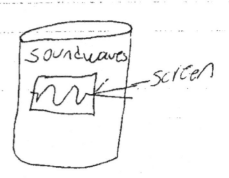

soundwaves
screen

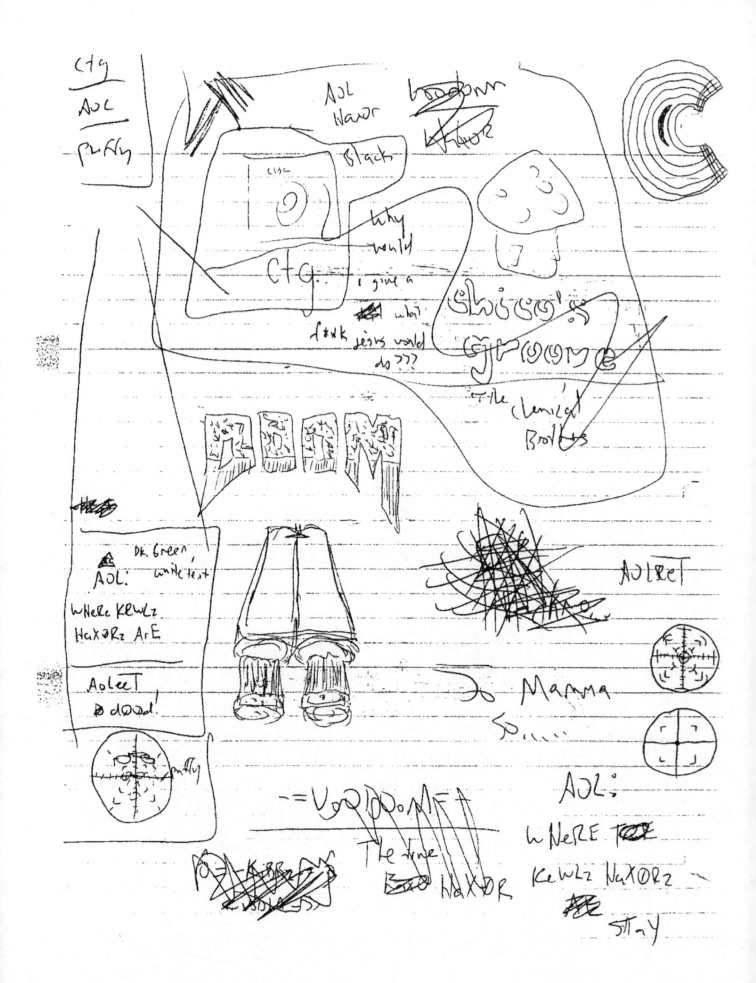

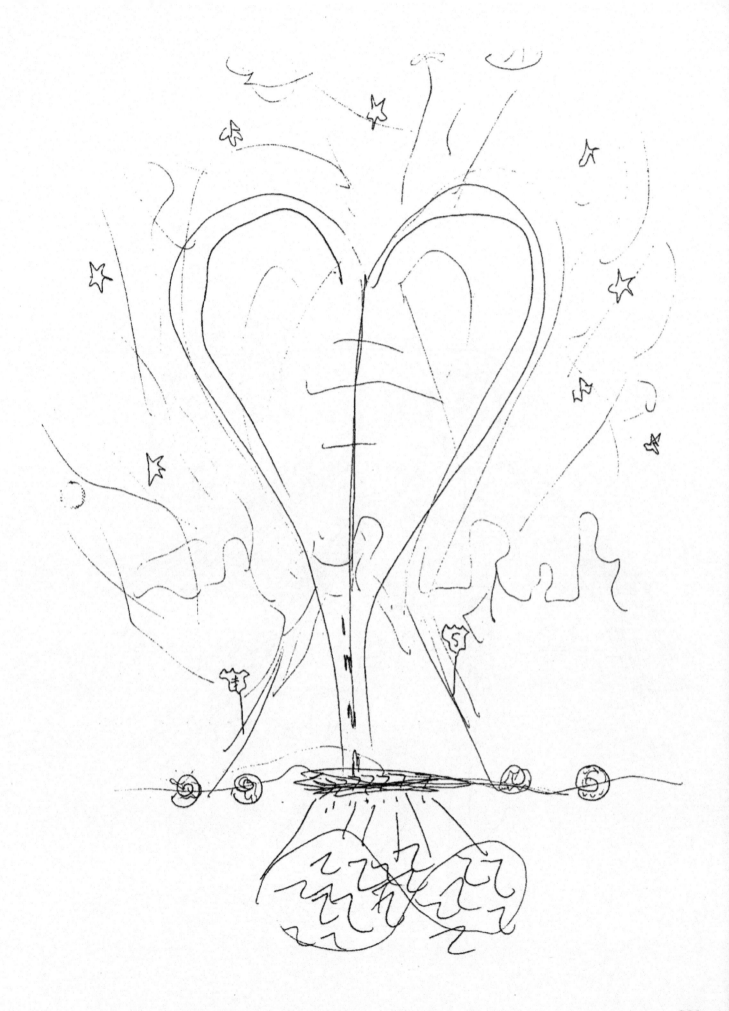

So Mamma → Philp

rappers, others

Some ol'

~~Hate~~ → Black Sunshine
— pissed off guy, knife, others

~~Love = Archie...exhaust...cars & driving...Hit it, shit, Cheez, weapons, explosives (or fast)~~

Hate = Liars, punk fags, bitches who hang w. them, commercials, faggots at work ███, people who hang in songs & think their kool, NBC, The WB, r movie checkers, Socks, grammar, Alt-███ mus, Age limits, taxes, Pussy Rap, Martial artists, Laid Back people, prices of stereo shit, ~~people~~ Rich people, annoying people, Speed limits, salesman, Charity commercials, wannabe experts of stuff, ~~teach~~ fag teachers, Star wars fags, Stupid people, Fass...fm of retards, popular lame ass sitcoms, ~~████~~ Assorted people, NPR, paparazzi's, enquirer mags, Rich lake people, HWF fans, cops, curfew laws, ~~████~~ celebrity benefits, Fuckers that say My kick ass cause ONLY their strong, welfare poachers, laser talkers, HANSON, JTT, thats all (Tommy hilfiger)

lawyers, psychiatrists,

racists
wannabe comedians,
people who act
as stolen to
chicks,
lawsuits,
some constitutional rights,
sexists, selfish people,
trends, fashions

Pics of groups
Descriptions, lists, links

Techno   Black Rockin Beats

— Something I can now make

Lyrics — Lists of All songs w. good lyrics

Pics

[Hacking] → Particle man

Summary of ALL fas warez & Hacking

computers, others

[CooLios] → sweet dreams

List of everyone,
Their pages, possibly mail stor

B&Butthead
Beuis   pics others

disarm [scribbled out]

(my Thoughtz)

Everything you wanna
tell about relsion, philo, etc.
              pentagram,   commandment tablets
Picz = [scribbled], [scribbled],
        [scribbled], peace symbol
        Anarchy

   &   ‡ - explain   I stay away [scribbled out]

[Other Cool MUS] →

Tell all other groups - non-techno
         you like

Pics = NIN, others of music

[Movies] → little gerr
                     Bc 1

explain good movies

Pics = resdoss, others

Its cool to hate.

~~Lets ~~

~~kill them all~~

woo - HAH! got you all in check

~~~~

~~~~

you what i have ??? yeea!

Fuck you AND yo mutha fuckin

So I Fut yo BItch

So mamma

So ......

Jeeeeaa!

. fat
. stupid
. ugly
. old
. bald

Dylan Klebold   9-11-81   ███████████████   ██████████

Eric & I were driving home (him driving his car), & we
stopped at the parking lot thingy at Deer Creek rd & Wadsworth.
We got out, & he set off a few fireworks, & then we were going
around smashing bottles. Then almost at the same time, we both got the
idea of breaking into this white van, which was something for an
electrical (maybe) company. We hoped to get the stuff inside. I put
on a snow glove, & then tried to punch through the passenger window. I tried
like 4 times & then Eric tried a couple times. We then found a
rock & I tried to break the window with that. After about 5 times,
the rock broke through, & I unlocked the door from the inside, & took
electrical stuff (& other things) — (don't know exactly), & then speed off
to Deer Creek open space park. We parked, & turned on the dome
light to see what we had. Then an officer saw us, got all that
we had, & then went thru the process. (arresting).

[signature]

Discovery Class

I attended the I.S.A.E discovery class on December 12, 1998.
This was an all-day class, instead of the four 2-hour class
option. I chose the all day at once method because I understand
things quickly. The class, truthfully, was not worth my time.
If I wasn't me, I would be voicing a different opinion. The
teacher was informative, and the information was valuable, but
I already knew almost all of what the teacher had to say. She
talked about influences, and how they affect us. Family,
friends, media T.V., radio almost everything around us is an
influence. I already knew this. She pointed out that influences
make us sometimes act differently. I knew that too. Our class
also talked about how to get what we wanted out of life. This is
by making positive, right choices and also by persevering toward
these goals. We talked about coping mechanisms. A coping
mechanism is what one uses to handle/manage stress, or how to
deal with problems. Some of these include counting, exercising,
taking a walk, reading, and many other tasks. A coping mechanism
is a positive alternative to making a wrong decision. I,
unfortunately for my boredom, knew these things too, and use
them and have used them on a regular basis for quite some time.
For the other kids in the class, however, this is a valuable
tool for them to use in their lives. The class talked about
values, and what was valuable to each of us. Some of the topics
that came up were friendship, knowledge, family, money, respect,
health, happiness, love, pleasure, and others. I, as any other
person, value these things too. The teacher linked these values
to the crimes we committed and the way we depleted these values
by commiting crime. I think this came thru to most of the people
in the class. And again, I already knew my values. All in all,
the class was a waste of time for me, and even though it went
over important skills that would be greatly beneficial to
someone else hearing them for the first time, it was an eight
hour day of pointless review and cramped conditions. I feel that
I shouldn't have had to take that class; but I'm just trying to
get out of the diversion program, as evidenced by my reluctant
attendance to this fit-for-an-uneducated-person's class.

time management

time management is an essential aspect of society in the twentieth century. since the invention of clocks in the middle ages, people have become more productive, efficient, and have had better life styles. knowing how and when to do certain things is one key to a happy lifestyle.

some examples of controlled time management are the daylight savings hour switching every spring and fall, and also the designated time for people to sleep. since we sleep at night, when doing work is not feasible because of the lack of sunlight, we can utilize the entire day for consciousness, when we can be as productive as possible. time management is a skill that some people have trouble obtaining, but these people, like me, can find ways of making useful time management schedules. every species integrates effective time management into its society, its survival. predators know to hunt at night, when other nocturnal animals will be active. the bear successfully uses time management, as he hibernates during the cold months of winter. without time management, productivity is decreased dramatically, sometimes to certain doom. in a seventeenth century battle during the seven years' war, the french had established a impenitratable stronghold on british land, a veritible beachhead for further invasion. the french cannons dug in, and the british had to retaliate. their final maneuver would be to scale the cliff walls opposite the cannons. the french general knew that a small british force was climbing these cliff walls but he expected the main army to come from the pass where the cannons were ready. he ordered soldiers to wheel the cannons and destroy the cliff scaling british, but this general waited. it turned out that the entire army climbed the cliff walls, breaking the french citadel and securing the land from any further invasion. "as i looked upon the bodies drying in the sun, i knew that he who hesitates is lost". this general did not know time management, as he hesitated when he should have acted. an experienced time management connaisieur would have rotated the cannons sooner, ending the british threat. in conclusion, this and other examples show the importance of time management.

I know its never everything

is true ...
my love is
same.

love ...

existence for
ever is the
happiness that
we have achieved
we cannot go

where is she...

forever I will wander,
neither, here nor, be with
her, (search to find) which gets

sadness pain,
eternal denial is known
when she doesn't love me...

I'm sorry

sorry

sadness
NIN
X

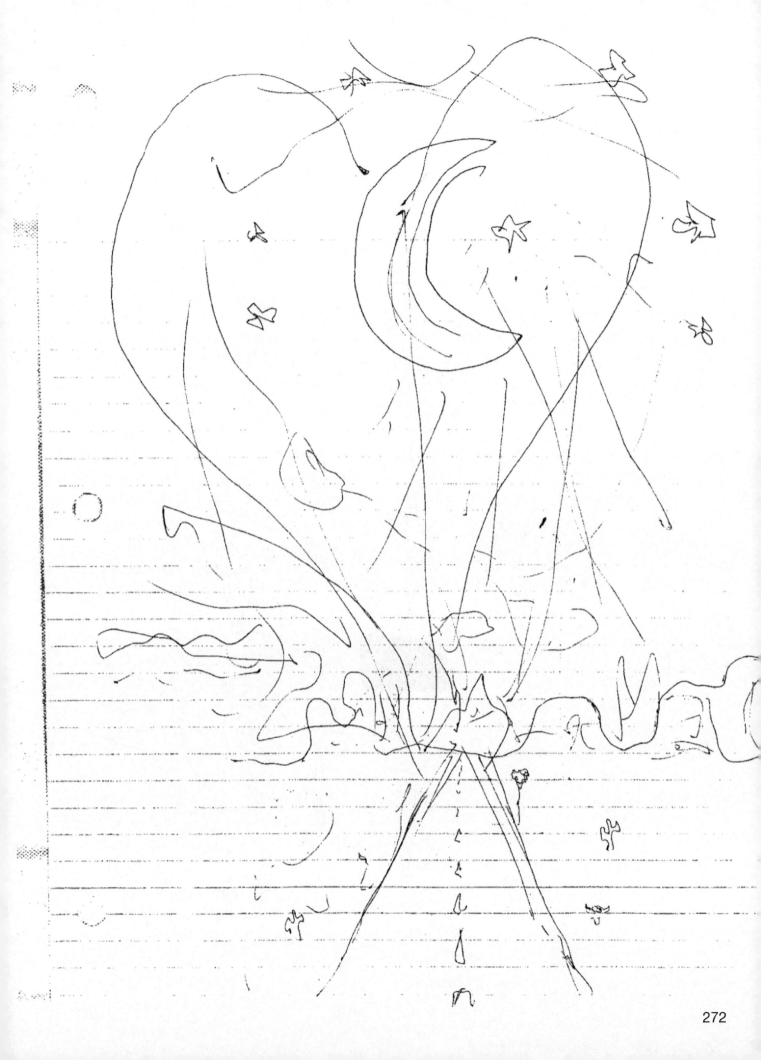

I now know the final battle, the pain of humanity is our love

I love you

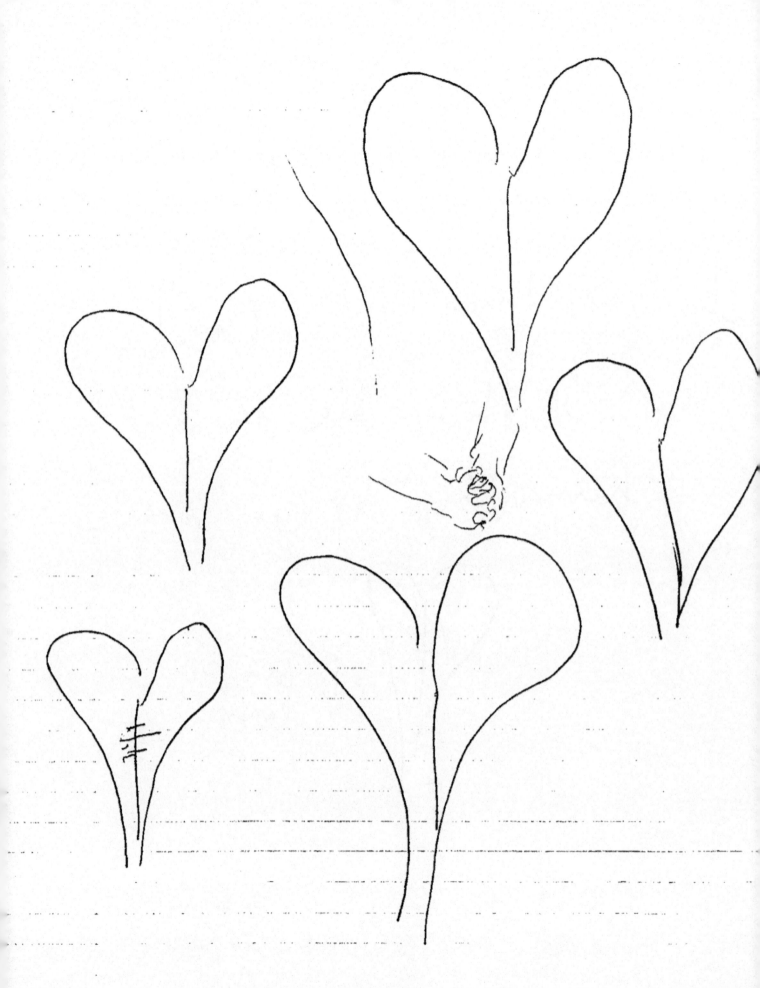

██████ is for the ████████████ joy
she gives me

██████ is for ~~the~~ how she ████████████
me helpless with her beautiful
smile.

██████ is for the ~~██████~~ ████████████
moments ~~time~~ she shares w/ me

██████ is for the ████████ kind
love that i've been looking for
all my life

██████ ~~is that~~ ████████ is the ████████
of us as a couple.

██████ = How ~~████~~ ~~██████~~ to   I hope
spend time with her

██████ = how she is the ████████
one i love, that i have ever loved

██████ = ~~████████████████~~ is for
the ████████ ~~████~~ where we can
look at the stars ████████ beautiful

██████ = How ████████████ she is

██████ = ~~her~~ ████ ~~for~~ everything
she does

To my love:

As a man, a conqueror does this deeds of greatness, He thinks he is complete. Yet, the true great person achieves happiness only when he has met ~~the~~ his soulmate: ~~the~~ Alone unknown until the first time they lay eyes on eachother. A true love is hard to come by, yet the most fulfilling, beautiful, completing achievement any man can have. Some have wealth, some have power, some have great intellect yet, I feel an infinant # of times greater than those, as I have found my true love.

My whole existence is flawed...
You get me closer to god..... (NIN)

Self-awareness...
Infinince.....
Existence.....
Knowledge.....
Neutrality.....
Possibility of Happiness....
Understanding of the everything.....

The candle burns,....
the stars set the
mood..... the
smoke fills the room....
the tope is set
then infinite places
all of purity...

NBK

Please don't show this note to
anyone.... it was meant only for
you.

(Don't tell anyone) either

(You know me...)

&??

If you don't know who I am I still, then I apparently haven't been noticeable enough... please don't take offense or worry about this note... if you do know who I am, or if you want to anyway, ~~scribbled~~ please leave a note in my locker saying whatever you want whether that be telling me to fuckoff or else you'll call the cops or if you want to say whatever, just please do me that favor... if you tell me to leave you alone, I will.

I like you ▓▓▓▓, but I won't force that ever.

#837

17-37-9

ps (I DID try to call you but you must have been asleep.)

(S)HITLIST

DO SHIT FOR NBK

File off clip.
Buy suspenders.
Buy cargo pants
work out carrying gear plan
Find out how to carry TEC-9
Get pouches - geologist in yer old closet.
Get napalm containers
Buy straps
Figure out how to carry knife
Practice in-car gearups
Get bullets
Get shells - .00
Give Reb powder
Buy Adidas soccer bag(s)
Give Reb glass containers
Fill up gascans
Find volatile combo. of gas & oil
Look for voltage amplifier, Intimed or Radioshak
Buy "wrath" Tshirt
Buy punk gloves.

BDAY shit

clips on
BP strap

crickets

bullets
shells
poison

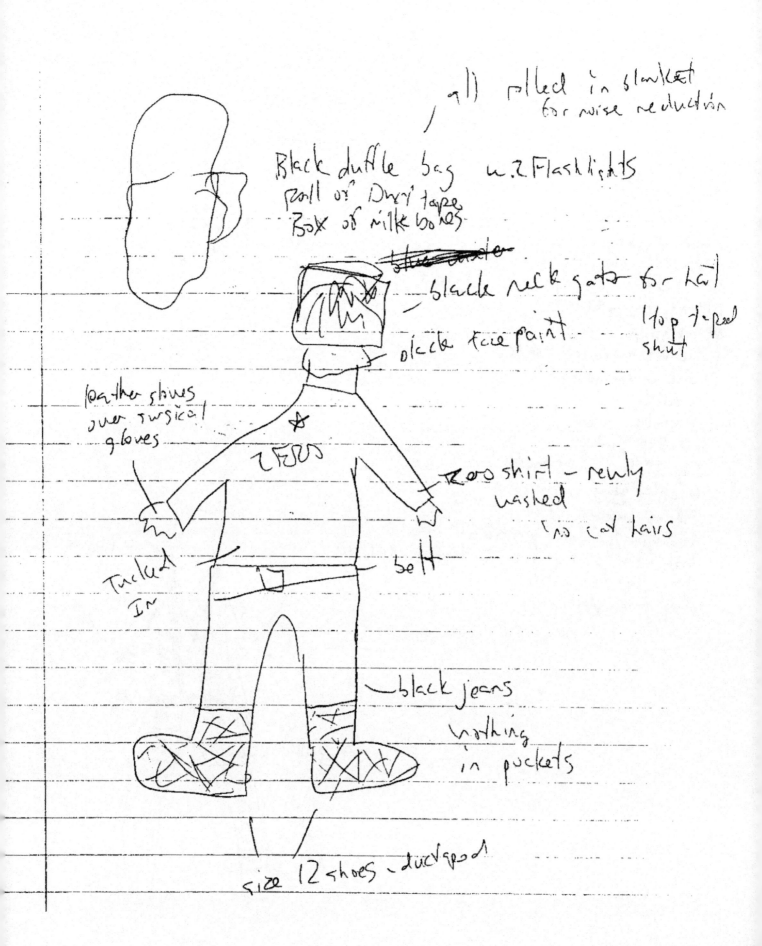

all rolled in blanket
for noise reduction

Black duffle bag   w. 2 Flashlights
roll of Duct tape
Box of milk bones

black neck gator for hat
top taped
shut

black face paint

leather gloves
over surgical
gloves

ZEROS

zoo shirt - newly
washed
no cat hairs

Tucked
In

belt

black jeans

nothing
in pockets

size 12 shoes - duct good

Full shit : (Needs fill)

Finger armor - right middle

~~(armor) Pistol~~

Uzi 9M

~~[illegible]~~

2 calicos

~~[illegible]~~

Flask

The humanity of here & now clouds all that
i see, yet the me, the one, can now control
the pain, & it is done. 5 more days. <u>5</u>
    A very influential number, another brick in my
journeyed wall. Humans are zombies, they scratch
for acceptance & greed & kill themselves
thru eachother. They will never learn, or maybe
they will, but wont have the strength to learn.
to be aware is not a trait, its a godlike thing.
Blessed be2. not a christian, jesus, not, sarai,
Abraham, David, bible gay shit god, but a true
controller of existence. was to make us this way.

These moments will be lost in the depressions
& covers of the human books forever, like, tears, in,
rain, but the thoughts will be eternal. To explain
the happiness is impossible even for fate, its just
a pure halcyon set to last more existences than
a conceivable number. Stupid gay nigger humans think
im "crazy" or they think im childish. hahaha, because
i cant solve $\int \sin^5 2x \cos^3 x \, dx$. That makes me dumb!
Because i cant staff thinking in a 2nd dimension, i go
to the 5th! haha so i wait 5 more days. 5 more days.
5 eternitys, & i know her & i are all concieved from
ourselves & eachother. every night of the self-awareness

284

journey, every thought we conceived, we have finished the race. time to die. everything we knew we were able to understand it, to perceive it, into what we should, everything we knew, we know & use, ~~scribbled~~ an understanding of the everything. An einstein stuck in an ant's body, we are the nature of existence. the zombies were atlest to see if our love was genuine. we are in merit of our reward, each other, the zombies will never cause us pain anymore. the humanity was a test. I love you love. Time to die, time to be free, time to love.

1 one day, one is the beginning, ? the end. hahaha. reversed, yet true. About 26.5 hours from now the judgement will begin. Difficulty but not impossible, necessary, nervewracking & fun.

What fun is life without a little death?

It's interesting, when i'm in my human form, knowing i'm going to die. Everything has a touch of triviality to it, like how none of this calculus shit matters the way it shouldn't. the truth. In 26.4 hours i'll be dead, & in happiness. the little zombie human bags will know their errors, & be forever suffering & mournful, HAHAHA of course i will miss things. not really.

WILL

Ok, this is my will. This is a fucking human thing to do but whatever.

███ — You were a badass, never failed to get me up when i was down. Thx. You get

FIRST

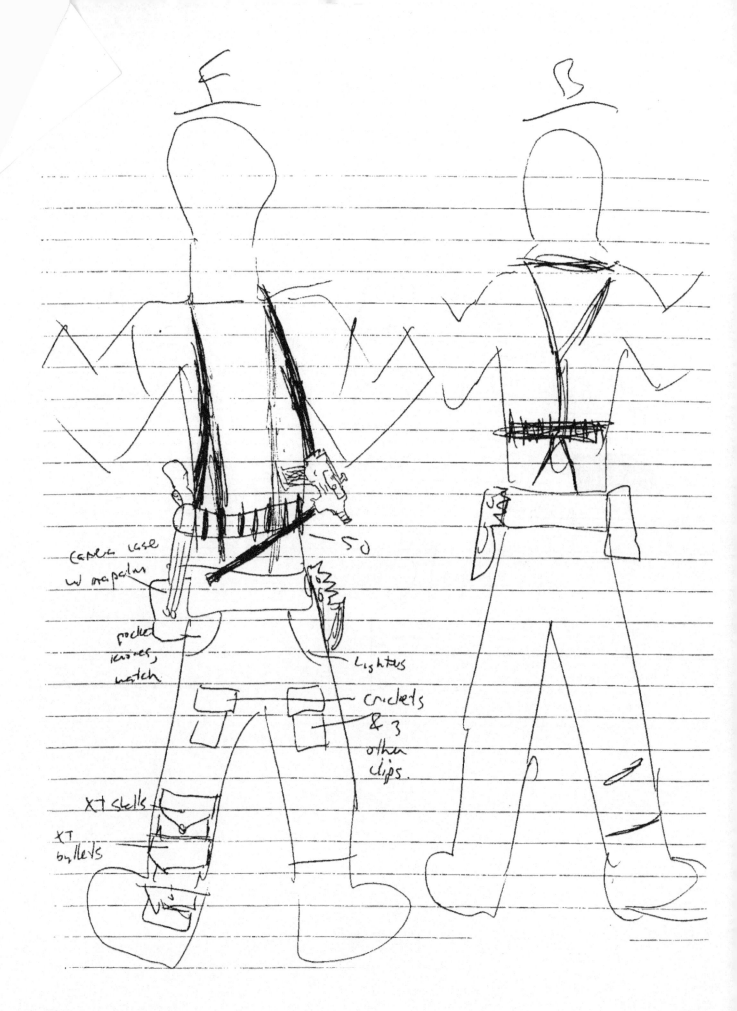

walk in, set bombs at 11:09, for 11:17
leave, set car bombs.
Drive to clement park. Gear up.
Get back by 11:15
Park cars. set car bombs for 11:18
get out, go to outside hill, wait.
when first bombs go off, attack.
have fun!

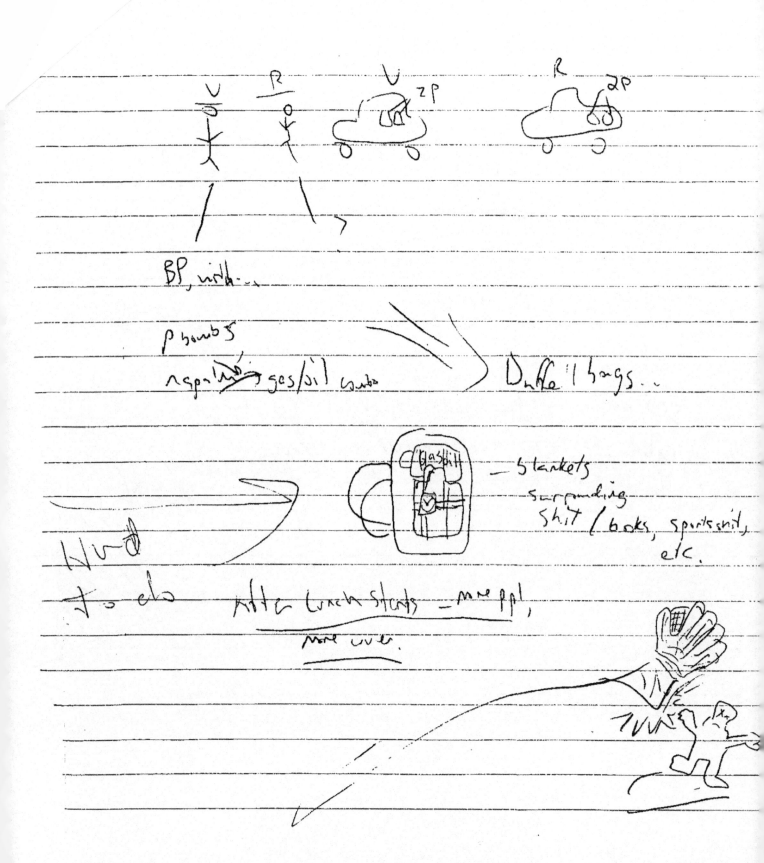

BP, with...

p bombs

~spilling ges/oil combo → Duffel bags...

glass shit

— blankets
surrounding
shit / books, sports shit,
etc.

Wud
to do   After Lunch starts — more ppl,
more cover.

Printed in Great Britain
by Amazon